250+
ACTIVITIES
AND
IDEAS
FOR
DEVELOPING
LITERACY
SKILLS

M. ELLEN JAY AND HILDA L. JAY

NEAL-SCHUMAN PUBLISHERS, INC.
NEW YORK   LONDON

Published by Neal-Schuman Publishers, Inc.
100 Varick Street
New York, NY 10013

Copyright © 1998 by M. Ellen Jay and Hilda L. Jay

Printed and bound in the United States of America.

Library of Congress Cataloging-in-Publication Data

Jay, M. Ellen.
    250+ activities and ideas for developing literacy skills / M. Ellen Jay, Hilda L. Jay.
        p. cm.
    Includes bibliographical references and index.
    ISBN 1–55570–329–1
    1. Language arts (Early childhood) 2. Literacy. 3. Early childhood education—Activity programs. 4. Reading (Early childhood) 5. Signs and symbols—Study and teaching (Early childhood) I. Jay, Hilda L., 1921–   . II. Title.
LB1139.5.L35J386   1998
372.6—dc21   98–16512
                                                         CIP

Contents

7 SCIENCE   93

8 GEOGRAPHY   109

9 ECONOMICS   133

10 COMPUTERS   145

Preface

DEFINING LITERACY

Traditionally, literacy has been equated with the ability to read and write words, inferring the ability to gain meaning from the written word. Sometimes the definition of literacy is extended to include the ability to use numbers.

The authors prefer what they believe to be a more useful definition, which broadens the standard one to include the ability to gain meaning from a wide variety of symbols and to understand the messages the symbols are intended to convey. This expanded definition includes the ability to interpret symbols used in such means of communication as pictures, maps, charts, graphs, mathematical or musical notations, and computer icons.

Since it is through literacy that one gains meaning, it is essential that these skills be introduced at an early age. Success in school, as well as in later life, requires that individuals be effective users of information, that they able to gather meaning from symbols. The ability to interpret symbols is a learned skill that can be acquired through play and through activities connected to daily routines and family life. Parents, teachers, and other interested adults can contribute significantly to this process. *250+ Activities and Ideas for Developing Literacy Skills* is intended to be a source of such activities.

Young children who are given experiences with symbols and learn to interpret them have a major advantage as they enter and move forward in school. The acquisition of such literacy skills allows the child to absorb the content being presented in the classroom. Without these skills the child is unable to generate meaning out of what the classroom teacher is saying or asking to be done. Frequently it is assumed that the students have acquired these skills intuitively, or that they are automatically acquired in connection with ongoing classroom activity and do not need to be taught directly. Thus, the child who, for whatever reason, is slow to comprehend these concepts is going to be at a major disadvantage in the classroom setting.

The greatest inequities among children entering school are linked to the presence or lack of background experiences, to their recognition of and ability to deal with divergent cultures, and to the degree of their development of emergent literacy. The smoothest transition from home to school will take place for those children who are the best prepared to meet classroom expectations.

ABOUT THIS BOOK

250+ Activities and Ideas for Developing Literacy Skills is intended to assist individuals who want to help children develop literacy skills as envisioned in the expanded definition of literacy. The activities presented here are designed for use by parents or other relatives with their own children, by day-care providers, by Head Start teachers, by classroom teachers, by public librarians, or by anyone else interested in giving children quality learning experiences.

Activities for All Types of Literacy

The Table of Contents reflects the authors' wider definition of literacy. The Introduction provides a philosophical foundation for fostering literacy skills. An understanding of this foundation is critical for success in using the book's activities with young children. The remainder of the book contains more than 250 activities that foster literacy skills. These activities are clustered around seven literacy types: linguistic, visual, math, science, geography, economic, and computer skills. Because of the extensiveness of linguistic literacy, Chapters 1–4 are devoted to the language arts— listening, reading readiness, beginning reading, and beginning writing. Since these four facets are closely intertwined, one can rarely compartmentalize them completely. The authors have used this grouping to facilitate the access and recognition of the unique attributes of each facet. The activities in Chapters 5–11 encourage the development of visual, math, science, geographic, economic and computer literacy skills.

Format of the Activities

The titles of the activities identify their content thrust. The activities are arranged according to increasing difficulty under the literacy heading with which they are associated. These activities should be used in any order that suits the adult and matches the child's readiness. The authors do not expect the users to follow through doing every activity in the order presented, or to complete one literacy activity list before engaging in easier activities from other literacy lists. The design of each activity is the same. The format includes

- the name or subject of the activity;
- prerequisite skills the child needs to be comfortable with before engaging in the activity;
- concepts that are to be learned by doing the activity;
- materials that the adult will need to assemble for use with the child;
- step-by-step procedures to follow; and
- extensions that provide for continued growth through expanded or more sophisticated activities.

Materials indicated in the activities with specific names (such as book titles) are merely suggestions. They will work well if they can be obtained. The problem is that sometimes materials go out of print, are revised, or are unavailable for other reasons. It is recommended that the adult work closely with a school or children's librarian at the public library. Should the titles sought not be in the local collection, these professionals can borrow the titles from another library through interlibrary loan. Also, these professionals should be able to suggest additional as well as alternative titles if the ones requested are unavailable. New materials are produced constantly and added to the collections with which these people are familiar. Their suggestions will supply materials the adult can use effectively with the child when introducing new concepts or reviewing concepts previously covered. Your best friend in these adventures is your librarian.

The authors encourage you to not only use these activities to foster literacy skills but also to share with young children a love of reading and learning—both the skills and the passion for knowledge and imagination will last a lifetime.

Introduction

The social, emotional, and cognitive development of children is influenced by the significant adults in their lives. What takes place in children's lives before they start formal public education has a great impact on their ability to learn in school and how they respond to opportunities. The child who has experienced the satisfaction of learning something of interest, of developing a skill, and of being valued is less likely to become labeled "at risk." Often the critical determining factor is the intervention of a significant adult, who may be the parent or another relative, day-care provider, babysitter, neighbor, or other caregiver.

WHO CAN USE THESE ACTIVITIES?

No one should believe that only those persons who have advanced degrees and formal training in education can provide the nurturing environment that is so beneficial to a child. Neither does one need a huge financial outlay to provide useful learning materials and experiences. Given three requirements, parents, the community at large, the public library, and other service organizations, can carry out literacy activities. The first of these requirements is an attitudinal outlook that recognizes the potential learning value found in everyday situations. The second is valuing the child as a person and having time to interact with the child. The third requirement is making quality use of the time spent interacting with the child. By observing what the child does and says—by picking up on things that are of interest to the child—one can learn to recognize what may be a developing interest of the child and, following these leads, one can foster learning. Observing the environment around the child to discover an interesting bug, the crack in the sidewalk, a newly issued stamp—each provides an opportunity to initiate conversations with the child. Including the child in food preparation, gardening, recycling, manipulating tools like scissors or hammers—provides the adult opportunities to introduce concepts and the child a chance to master them. Shared reading of books and viewing of television programs, videotapes, and CD-ROMs leads to discussion of ideas and issues.

The child who has contact on a daily basis with this type of adult role model will develop similar sets of values and attitudes. The child who has experienced the joy of discovery, the pleasure of satisfying one's curiosity, the fascination of discussing ideas, and the delight in listening to someone read aloud has significant advantages over the child who has not had these experiences.

HOW DO THESE ACTIVITIES HELP FOSTER LITERACY?

In an effort to provide the best preparation for learning and schooling, however, it is important not to "push" the child into developmentally inappropriate activities. Forcing children to practice writing before their maturity and fine motor skills are sufficiently developed can delay and and even hinder achieving the goal. Physical skills develop in sequence. When attempting to negotiate stairs, the child starts by placing both feet on a single step. Later as the child grows and develops skill, one foot is placed on each step. Similarly, one can see the development of balance when the child can stand on one foot, or stand and walk on tiptoes. Further development is indicated when the child can walk forward and backward with eyes closed. In time, walking on a balance beam becomes possible. Jumping begins by using both feet together and moves to hopping on one foot and finally skipping. Ball-handling skills proceed from kicking to bouncing to catching and throwing. The desire to pull or push a small toy leads to doing the same thing with a wagon. The use of a pedal car, tricycle, and bicycle follow upon each other. Fine-motor skills also develop as a result of practice. There are books and other devices for the very young that let them button, zip, lace, tie, buckle, and Velcro.™ These skills can be reinforced in the context of dressing and changing clothes. Play activities such as stacking blocks and threading beads help develop eye hand coordination and improve fine-motor skills. Closely related to early school success is the use of drawing and writing materials, scissors, and paste or glue. Experience with thick markers and crayons leads to use of standard pencils and pens. Learning to cut with scissors and control glue presents additional challenges.

Just as there is a developmental level necessary to succeed with physical skills, there is a similar match needed between developmental level and success with cognitive skills. Until a child can say the letters of the alphabet, pair letter names with the symbols, and match the sound to the letter, reading cannot take place. In mathematics it is necessary to establish number concept and pair the number with its symbol before learning basic math facts. The difficult thing for the adult to recognize is when the child is developmentally ready to be introduced to more challenging activities. The trick is to encourage steady growth while retaining an element of fun and limiting frustration.

Some of the most recent brain research only re-emphasizes the need for interaction with the child—from the moment of birth. Although the brain continues to develop through adult life, its periods of rapid development are at the beginning. Those educators who have complained that young children are capable of much more than is often expected of them now have increased support. Indeed, there is evidence that once the optimal time for learning a given type of skill is passed, it becomes many times more difficult and time consuming to acquire it.

Current research suggests that there is a dual role in the creation of the mind: the genes are responsible for the brain's main circuits, while circuits that appear to be developed after birth are dependent upon environment. When one looks at the microscopic views of brain tissue, the complexity of the connections made by the brain's one hundred billion neurons is overwhelming. Using the analogy of computer linkage, Sharon Begley writes that

> a baby's brain is a jumble of neurons, all waiting to be woven into the intricate tapestry of the mind. Some of the neurons have already been hard-wired, by the genes in the fertilized egg, into circuits that command breathing or control heartbeat, regulate body temperature or produce reflexes. But trillions upon trillions

more are like the Pentium chips in a computer before the factory preloads the software. They are pure and of almost infinite potential, unprogrammed circuits that might one day compose rap songs and do calculus, erupt in fury and melt in ecstasy. If the neurons are used, they become integrated into the circuitry of the brain by connecting to other neurons; if they are not used, they may die. It is the experiences of childhood, determining which neurons are used that wire the circuits of the brain as surely as a programmer at a keyboard reconfigures the circuits in a computer. Which keys are typed—which experiences a child has—determines whether the child grows up to be intelligent or dull, fearful or self-assured, articulate or tongue-tied. (Begley 1996: 56).

AT WHAT AGE SHOULD THESE ACTIVITIES BE USED?

Finding that there are time limits, "windows of opportunity," in which to learn specific skills, calls for rethinking the operation of schools. And since these time periods are placed at the earliest end of life, the role of the adult in the baby's initial (preschool) years becomes even more demanding and important.

Infants acquire recognition of the sounds of language phonemes within their first year, according to researcher Patricia Kuhl. She holds that "by 12 months infants have lost the ability to discriminate sounds that are not significant in their language, and their babbling has acquired the sound of their language." (Begley 1997: 57). These findings explain why the older you get the more difficult it becomes to learn a foreign language —to master sounds that were ruled out in your first year of life. Vocabulary develops rapidly in the first two years. The more words the child knows, the greater the range of the adult vocabulary. A child needs to be talked to and encouraged to listen actively.

Music also takes root around age three, and German research indicates that the younger the child begins playing an instrument the larger the amount of somatosensor cortex dedicated to the thumb and fifth finger of the left hand—the fingering hand of string players. According to this research the circuits formed early in life, including those for music, endure.

Math logic and higher order thinking also respond to early shaping experiences. This does not mean that all schooling should be pushed down indiscriminately, but it does mean that the preparatory and developmental efforts should be put in place so that the child has the tools needed to succeed in school. We cannot afford to overlook that the brain neurons are being shaped and locked into place from day one. The child does not have "lots of time" ahead to learn and experience, if the researchers are correct and there are limited "windows of opportunity" in which to acquire base learning. The child needs parental (adult) attention, the opportunity to experience speech and thought, to be talked and sung to, to become involved in play and games, to gain a sense of number, and to become challenged by problems to solve. The activities suggested in this book are meant to help the adult initiate activities and to encourage sharing them with young children in an atmosphere of fun and games.

Traditionally, a school curriculum includes learning to read, using numbers, writing, and the study of the various disciplines. Providing readiness experiences makes the transition to the formal classroom learning easier and more productive. The child who arrives at school with concepts of print and numbers; with experience in observing such relationships as cause and effect, same and different, patterns and sequences; and with practice in expressing ideas and opinions will feel comfortable in the school environment and will be less likely to experience the anxiety and frustration factors that inhibit learning.

Although much of what is presented in this book relates to preschool activity, the nurturing and supportive nature of adult interaction must not stop once the child enters school. The teaming of the home and the school provides continuity for the child. When expectations of the child differ significantly, the child becomes confused and does not prosper. The school can provide experiences that rely on group interaction and instructional materials rarely available in homes, but the home should still expect to enrich and augment what is learned in the group setting. While the classroom teacher is expected to expand individual learning, the overriding focus of accountability is the need to ensure the progress of the entire class.

WHAT TYPES OF ACTIVITIES ARE IN THIS BOOK?

The activities in *250+ Activities and Ideas for Developing Literacy Skills* are clustered around seven types of literacy: linguistic, visual, mathematic, scientific, geographic, economic, and computer. Within these clusters, activities range from introductory to exploratory. The user will observe that there is great interrelatedness among these literacies,

literacies, the behaviors used to develop proficiencies, and the materials used. Acquisition of literacies does not follow a linear progression in which the child masters all visual literacy skills before being introduced to economic or geographic literacy. Within each literacy there is a hierarchy of skills to be worked through in order to develop proficiency, but, there is no similar hierarchy among the literacies. Introductory activities related to each of them should be experienced before attempting to master any given literacy. The approach needs to be cyclical, revisiting each literacy as maturity and readiness increase.

The process of sharing a book with a child, for example, allows the adult to introduce concepts related to visual literacy through a discussion of the illustrations; to present concepts of print related to reading readiness; and to review the book's subject matter to foster content literacy such as science, geography, or economics. The same multifaceted benefits arise from sharing television viewing and discussing hands-on activities. It is not possible to completely compartmentalize information or interactions. Interrelationships become evident when one recognizes that the acquisition of content information requires the ability to interpret visual, textual, and numerical symbols. Similarly, one discovers that there are no distinct boundaries between content areas. For example, the study of weather and climate contains both scientific components and geographic components. The science of weather focuses on fronts, differences in air pressure, the water cycle, the formation of storms, and so forth. Specific weather and climate depend on geographic location.

Other common threads that weave through all of the literacies and need development are listening skills and thinking skills. It is frequently assumed that because a child hears something that listening is taking place. This assumption is invalid. The development of listening skills is frequently overlooked and deserves increased attention. Listening requires considerably more than just "hearing." It requires dealing with the complexities of grasping and understanding what is said, especially if what is being said incorporates ideas new to the listener. It also requires dealing with the natural resistance to listening when what is being said expresses ideas that differ substantially from our own. If the person is angry or scared, if the topic has intense emotional or personal importance for the listener, or if the listener has a closed mind, much that is said can be missed. Listening is more difficult still when the listener wants to break in with comment or rebuttal of his/her own. When we assume that we are correct we do not listen carefully to dissenting evidence—or we tend to discount it or adapt it so that it is less threatening to our own point of view. According to John Lewis in a discussion of voting and election-year listening to candidates, "There's something to be said for deliberation. If you're not sure what you think, you're likely to go on listening" (Mancini 1996: 24). It takes practice to avoid shutting off listening.

Everyone is guilty periodically of poor listening. In 1989, George Usova determined that as much as 90 percent of all communication was verbal, it was held that the average listener retained only about half of what had been said immediately after hearing the information. A few hours later the percentage retained had fallen to 20–25 percent. Schools may change in this regard, but it has been calculated that students spend 45 percent of their classroom time listening, but only 30 percent talking, 16 percent reading, and 9 percent writing (Usova 1989: 59). Even if schools change these instructional percentages as a result of integrating technology formats such as CD-ROMs, listening and reading skills will still be required.

Usova also points out that we need to realize that there is significant opportunity to listen and think while engaging in conversation. Consider that when two people converse, theoretically each will devote 50 percent of the time listening. When four people are involved, listening time increases to 75 percent. While this allows for more time to use listening and thinking skills, it also allows for more opportunities for distractions. The child can be helped to recognize that it takes effort to listen well and that the child is largely in control of that effort. Gradually the child accepts that the speaker's information can have personal worth, that it is also important to separate fact from fiction, and that the listener must examine the evidence offered for bias, logic, and reasonableness.

HOW CAN I MODEL LITERACY SKILLS WITH A YOUNG CHILD?

Thinking skills are necessary for problem solving and decision making. Young children experience decision-making and problem-solving situations every day, which illustrates the need to provide them with the skills to cope. The activities described later in this book will help the child develop and practice thinking skills through interaction with the environment. The recognition of relationships and making appropriate responses begin with things as simple as wearing a raincoat on a rainy day or choosing not to write on the wall. The adult can model thinking skills by verbalizing their own behaviors or identifying the good thinking skills used by a character in a storybook or television program, thus helping the child begin to appreciate the role of critical thinking. With increased experience, one comes to realize that what is not said, or information that is not provided, may have as much impact on the decision being made as the information that is provided. Recognition of the use of thinking skills by others encourages the child to begin applying these skills independently. The ability to evaluate the strengths and weaknesses of various options available is a lifelong skill. Too heavy an emphasis on rote learning and the recall of facts will not prepare a child for life in the information age. Experiences that involve locating, organizing, creating, evaluating, and sharing information are also needed to prepare the child for the future.

An adult who is involved with a child's development and is watching the child's growth may find it rewarding to continue the baby-book concept of recording and dating accomplishments. It is not a very large step from writing down first smile, first word, first step to recording descriptions of cognitive growth. Keep anecdotal descriptions of the child's "aha" experiences as learning occurs. Direct quotations, a portfolio of products, and video or audiotapes all document the child's development. These records can not only help the adult recognize and direct the child's growth, but they also may simply become a family treasure.

Chapter 1

Language Arts—Listening

A major source of information is the spoken word. Talking to young children serves many functions. Initially, it provides a model to mimic in the development of language, but soon it also serves to encourage verbal interactions which provide the answers to questions. The ability to listen and gain meaning from what is said is crucial for success in school. Fluency in using spoken language provides a foundation to build on when beginning to learn to transform verbal responses into the appropriate symbols used when learning to read and write.

RECOGNITION OF SOUNDS

Sounds, in addition to the spoken word, provide essential information for personal safety as well as clues for interacting with the world at large. Children who can identify objects and events by the sounds they make learn to take appropriate actions. Developing an awareness of the world of sounds and how to interpret them has many benefits.

Prerequisite Skills

- Ability to hear and differentiate attributes of sounds.

Concepts

- Sounds can be categorized.
- Sounds provide meaningful information.
- Sounds have different sources.

Materials

- A variety of sounds actual and/or recorded.

Procedures

- Help the child make connections between routine sounds and their meaning. Initial sounds would include a ringing telephone or doorbell, the opening or closing of a door, sounds related to moving traffic, animal sounds, running water, and the like.
- As the child becomes more skilled at identifying characteristics of sounds and their specific sources, the adult can foster more and more subtle discrimination. Have the child listen to sound-effects recordings or TV sound tracks and attempt to identify the source of a specific sound.
- Discuss appropriate reactions to specific sounds to help make these reactions become automatic.

Extensions

- While listening to recorded sounds, tell where one would be and describe what would be around you if you were actually hearing the sound.

MUSICAL SOUNDS

Listening to music provides pleasure. It can also provide practice in auditory discrimination in listening. Children should be exposed to a wide range of music, not just popular radio station broadcasts. Listening to tapes and CDs of children's songs and nursery rhymes helps a child develop the common background of cultural literacy and language development drawn upon in school. Exposing the child to classical and ethnic as well as popular music enables the child to learn to discriminate differences in style, rhythm, pitch, and sounds of instruments.

Prerequisite Skills

- Awareness of musical sounds and/or rhythm.

Concepts

- High and low pitch.
- Rhythmic patterns.
- Recognition of melody as a musical element.
- Musical notation permits replication.

Materials

- Recorded musical sounds.
- Live musical sounds.
- Samples of musical notation.

Procedures

- Provide shared listening experiences. Respond to the mood of the music with body movements.
- Have the child sing along with an adult or recordings.
- Encourage the child to match pitches vocally with a prompt such as piano, adult voice, guitar, autoharp, harmonica, and the like. Discuss high and low pitches and the direction of motion within a tune.
- Play or beat a rhythmic pattern and have the child attempt to match the prompt. As the child's coordination develops, increase the sophistication of the prompt.

Extensions

- Discover the dupal or triple nature of rhythms. Demonstrate clapping or moving to express the accented beat patterns and then have the child respond to the rhythms.
- Create homemade instruments to explore pitch, rhythm, and the role of vibration in sound production. Ones that are easy to construct include a drum, rubber-band guitar, wind chime, or softdrink bottle flute.

AUDITORY DISCRIMINATION

Auditory discrimination is essential for language development. Being able to hear the differences in pronunciation of letter sounds permits the development of clear speech and later enables the child to transfer this discrimination to written symbols.

Prerequisite Skills

- Ability to distinguish differences between sounds.
- Ability to produce specific verbal sounds.

Concepts

- Rhyming words share the same ending sound.
- The written letter symbol is connected to a spoken sound.
- Letter symbols may have more than one sound.

Materials

- Samples of easy printed material—picture books, ABCs, rhyming books.
- Mail-order catalogs that contain pictures which can be matched with initial consonant sounds.

Procedures

- As the child shows interest in matching the printed word with what is being read to them, begin to identify the sound/letter relationship.

- Have the child suggest words that begin with the same sound as a familiar word such as their name or common objects: Bill, book, boy, bat, ball, boat, and so forth.
- Start exploring examples of rhyming words. Create lists of word "families," for example: bat, cat, fat, sat; fit, hit, lit, mit, sit.
- Find examples of rhyming word patterns in stories and poems.

Extensions

- Explore examples of letters having more than one sound, such as long and short vowels, hard and soft consonants, and the effect of rules of phonics.
- Explore examples of diphthongs and consonant blends.
- Explore examples of homographs, in which words spelled the same way sound different when they have different meanings (bow of boat and bow in your hair).
- Explore homophones (or homonyms), in which the words sound the same but have different spellings for different meanings (to, too, two).
- Have fun with words whose sound is also its meaning (boom, snap, crack, etc.).
- Play word games in which sounds and patterns provide enjoyment.
- Introduce foreign language words.

PATTERN BOOKS

Some books have predictable, repeated phrases that allow the child to anticipate and participate in the reading of the stories. Encouraging the child to chime in when the phrase occurs encourages focused listening.

Prerequisite Skills

- Attention span for listening.
- Ability to recognize repetition.

Concepts

- There are times when it is appropriate to join in when someone is reading a story or singing a song.
- The repeated segment is a distinguishable unit.

Materials

- Stories that contain repeated phrases.
- Songs with repeated choruses.

Procedures

- Before reading the story, identify the pattern phrases and have the child practice repeating it.
- Read the story and invite the child to participate.
- As experience is gained with this type of story, encourage the child to discover and identify repeated patterns without having them pointed out.

Extensions

- Include chants and songs that have repeated choruses.
- Following the patterns, create additional verses or adventures to extend the songs or stories.

FOLLOWING VERBAL DIRECTIONS

Throughout life, the ability to follow verbal instructions is an essential skill. The child must learn to recognize when directions are being given, that directions need to be followed, and how to listen in order to comprehend them. These skills can be introduced and developed in the context of play. It is important to maintain consistency of expectation and follow-through to develop good habits and behaviors that aid the child in following directions. The child needs to be helped to differentiate between seemingly conflicting sets of directions, particularly in the area of personal safety. For example, parents direct children not to talk to or go with strangers yet a convincing adult asking them for their help creates a problem. The child also finds it difficult when parents and teachers provide conflicting directions. Parents often say it's OK to hit back while teachers say don't fight. Ultimately, the child must learn not to follow directions blindly, but develop the skills needed to determine appropriate directions to follow.

Prerequisite Skills

- Recognition of authority.
- Understanding cause and effect.

Concepts

- Understand one's role in the connection between behaviors and outcomes.
- There are times when one cannot change the sequence of actions because the order determines the outcome.
- Interpreting directions is enhanced by the recognition of clue words.
- Personal safety can depend on immediate response to directions.

Materials

- Cards with sample directions written on them for reference.

Procedures

- Start off by reviewing and then building on the child's experiences in following directions that are a necessary part of family life, such as come when called, stop doing something, pick up your toys, it's bedtime.
- In the context of play ask the child to perform specific tasks: go get the ball, touch your nose, point to an object.
- Progress to multiple-step tasks such as: go to a specific place, get something, and bring it back; on a piece of paper draw an object, circle it, and hold it upside down to show me.
- Play games such as "Simon Says" to provide the child with practice in discriminating cue words.
- Ask the child to identify the key words in a set of di-

rections and explain in their own words what is being asked for by the directions.

- Give the child experiences in verifying if the criteria asked for in the directions have been fulfilled, and then discuss whether the criteria have in fact been met. The ability to engage in self-monitoring, and the habit of doing so, are necessary skills.

Extensions

- Move on to interpreting written directions and making sure that they have been followed.
- Introduce strategies for remembering multistep directions.

DRAMATIC ROLE PLAYS

A child's participation in conversations encourages both speaking and listening. In addition to engaging in spontaneous conversation, spend time with the child role playing conversational interactions from daily life situations. You might pretend you are ordering food at a fast food restaurant, making a phone call to Grandma, buying a pair of shoes, filling the car with gas and paying for it, checking out a book at the library. These conversations are give-and-take situations in which the next response is based on what the person hears. The relationship between listening and responding is an important one to develop and requires practice.

Prerequisite Skills

- Experiences with conversations in a variety of settings.

Concepts

- People exchange information through conversations.
- A conversation requires the person to alternate between speaking (providing information) and listening (receiving information).
- Responses are adapted and revised based upon what is heard.

Materials

- A series of prompts to initiate conversations.
- Props to enhance dramatic role playing.

Procedures

- Select a situation to role play, suggest parts to be assumed, and act out the situation.
- Exchange roles and re-enact the situation.
- Explore additional conversational situations.

Extensions

- Build in some "error" in your responses so that the child must listen for meaning and correct misinformation as an integral part of the conversation.

MEANINGFUL QUESTIONING

Young children frequently ask questions for the fun of asking them without paying attention to the answer. Establishing such a habit is detrimental. The child needs to be guided toward making a connection between asking a question and listening to the answer. One strategy for encouraging good listening on the part of the child is for the adult to model such behavior. Insofar as is possible, make a point of stopping what one is doing to truly give attention to the child's conversation. Questions worth asking are worth listening to. The same is true for answers.

Prerequisite Skills

- The ability to recognize the relationship between asking a question and receiving its answer.

Concepts

- When a question is worth asking, the answer deserves being listened to.
- Inaccurate listening creates problems; misinformation leads to misunderstandings and mistakes.
- Recognize that there are appropriate and inappropriate situations for asking questions.

Materials

- Situations in which question asking and answering take place.

Procedures

- Make a point of analyzing question-and-answer reactions and discuss with the child the importance of listening to the answers to questions.
- Model good listening to encourage similar behavior in the child.

Extensions

- Discuss the principles of courtesy that are associated with asking questions and giving answers, such as not interrupting unless there is an emergency.
- Discuss how to structure questions so that they produce meaningful information in contrast to frivolous, attention-seeking questions.

Chapter 2

Language Arts—Reading Readiness

Reading readiness starts developing from day one. Both affective and cognitive components enter into readiness. Just as children learn to speak by copying the language patterns of those around them, they also develop an interest in reading from those around them. A child raised in a print-rich environment where reading is valued, in which they are read to, and in which they see others reading, will develop an interest in learning to read. When you share books with a child you help train many of their reading-readiness skills. Research supports the correlation between reading to a child and the child learning to read and being successful in school.

READING ALOUD

Reading aloud to a child provides much more than the enjoyment of time together and the storyline. While these are important parts of capturing the child's interest in books and reading, the adult modeling of the process introduces the child to the concepts that must be mastered in order to learn to read. Traditionally, when sharing a story discussions focus on who does what in the story. Elements of humor are enjoyed and illustrations are examined. Reading aloud also allows for introducing concepts of print that are essential to learning to read; for example: print contains a message, words are composed of letters and clusters of letters, one reads from left to right and progresses from top to bottom of the page, the left page is read before the right page. The adult can also demonstrate the appropriate care and handling of books by having clean hands, opening and closing the book gently, turning the page carefully, resisting the urge to mark them, and respectfully storing the book. These are behaviors that need to be practiced and should be part of being read to. Initial read-aloud experiences will have begun in infancy when the child's interaction with the story may be difficult to observe. An established routine of story reading progresses naturally into reading readiness.

Prerequisite Skills

- Have contact with a literate adult who is willing to read to the child.
- Sufficient attention span to listen to a book being read.

Concepts

- Listening to stories is enjoyable.
- One enjoys stories even more when they are shared with others.

- It's important to take good care of books.
- Recognize the relationship of print to the spoken word.

Materials

- Story books.

Procedures

- Establish a routine for story reading.
- Gradually involve the child in selecting the book to be read, discussing the story, and discovering concepts of print, book handling, and reading.

Extensions

- Start with simple, concrete, repetitive stories for the very young.
- Begin to introduce stories that reflect the child's own experiences, such as eating, having a friend, enjoying a pet, and bedtime.
- As the child's interests and abilities develop, select stories that mirror the child's own interests, such as dinosaurs, animals, transportation, machinery, and sports.

PARTS OF A BOOK

Children need to learn the vocabulary used in identifying the parts of a book. When talking about books with others, a shared vocabulary is necessary. These terms also form a base for directions frequently encountered in school settings.

Prerequisite Skills

- Concepts of front and back, inside and outside, up and down.
- There are names for things and parts of things.

Concepts

- Develop the following concepts: front and back covers, spine, pages, title page, dust jacket, text, illustrations.

Materials

- Wide range of picture and story books.

Procedures

- Examine books together and identify their parts.
- Use appropriate vocabulary when sharing books.
- Ask the child to point to or find specific parts.

Extensions

- Develop the concepts of table of contents, index, glossary, and end pages.

- Talk about what the author, illustrator, and publisher do, and the function of the copyright date.
- Discuss different media used to illustrate books—collage, photograph, drawing, painting, watercolor, woodcut—as you encounter them.

TOP TO BOTTOM, LEFT TO RIGHT

The child needs to recognize that there is a sequence followed when reading text. Readers of western languages move from top to bottom and left to right on a page, and they read the left page before the right. Letters in a word are also sequenced left to right. This consistency is necessary to provide universality in reading throughout contexts: book, letter, sign, billboard, license plate—any printed or written message.

Prerequisite Skills

- Up and down (top and bottom).
- Left and right.

Concepts

- When reading, one begins at the top of the page and ends at the bottom.
- One reads the left-hand page before the right-hand page.
- Within a single page, words are arranged in order and read left to right.

Materials

- Printed material from various sources.

Procedures

- When sharing stories with the child, indicate where you are starting to read.
- Sometimes mark with your finger where you are reading.
- Ask the child to indicate where to read next—for example, when a page is turned.

Extensions

- Introduce the idea that Asian and Arabic peoples read the page differently, and that the symbols we use look unfamiliar to them.
- Although they read from left to right, there are story books, such as *Round Trip* by Ann Jonas, that are bound so that they can be read front to back, then turned upside down and continued.

ALPHABET AND LETTER RECOGNITION

Research continues to show a strong connection between knowing letter names and later learning to read. Children can recite the alphabet before they attach names to letter forms. Once the individual letter symbol is connected to its name, the sounds it makes can also begin to be connected to the letter symbol. Another skill related to learning the alphabet involves learning the order of the letters sufficiently to begin at points within it and move forward and backward with ease. This becomes important when later in school the child must alphabetize and use guide words.

Prerequisite Skills

- An awareness of letters.

Concepts

- Individual letters have distinctive forms and names.
- There is a sequence to the letters of the alphabet.

Materials

- Alphabet books.
- Printed material in one's environment.
- Magnetic letters for use on the refrigerator door or other magnetic surface.

Procedures

- Use the alphabet song to familiarize the child with the letter names and their sequence.
- Practice identifying letters found around you in text, on signs, on the television screen, and in books, magazines, and newspapers.
- Give directions to the child to move magnetic letters to demonstrate recognition of specific letters and appropriate sequence such as find the d or spell cat.

Extensions

- Introduce the concept of upper and lower case letters.
- Encourage the child to draw letter forms.

SEQUENCE OF EVENTS IN A STORY

Comprehension of a story involves recognizing the sequence of events—what comes before and after. Sequencing is a thinking skill that can be practiced. The concept begins when the child can identify the beginning, middle, and the ending events. The degree of detail retained increases with maturity, practice, and exposure. The ability to retell a story verifies the child's understanding of the story.

Prerequisite Skills

- Sense of before and after.
- Knowing what an event is.
- Ability to identify events within a story.

Concepts

- Main idea and related supporting details.
- Chronological order.
- A summary provides a concise restatement of the main points.

Materials

- Stories to share.

- Use flannel-board pieces to represent the parts of a story being sequenced.
- Drawing materials.

Procedures

- Select and share a story with the child.
- Ask the child to retell the story using the child's own words, by using flannel-board pieces, or by drawing a sequence of pictures.
- Discuss omissions and incorrect sequences and the need for logic.

Extensions

- Ask the child to tell what might have happened before the start of the story and explain why.
- Ask the child to make a prediction and listen to verify its accuracy.
- Compare and contrast different versions of the same story such as *Jack and the Beanstalk* with *Jim and the Beanstalk*, or *Three Little Pigs* with *The True Story of the Three Little Pigs*, or *Goldilocks and the Three Bears* with *Somebody and the Three Blairs*.

RHYMING WORDS

Phonemic awareness involves recognizing initial and ending consonant sounds. Rhyming focuses on words with ending sounds that match. Once introduced to the concept of rhyme, children enjoy discovering it in the context of stories and games. When you introduce children to rhyme, you help them develop word-attack skills by varying initial consonants while retaining the rhyming feature of the word "family." For example, the "at" family produces bat, cat, fat, hat, mat, pat, rat, sat. Verbal games of this sort prepare the child for transition to printed text. As with other aspects of language, the ability to say and hear rhymes precedes the ability to read and write these words.

Prerequisite Skills

- Adequate auditory discrimination to enable the child to hear rhymes.
- Enjoyment of words.

Concepts

- Discriminate between beginning and ending sounds of words.
- Recognize rhyme as the similarity in word-ending sounds.
- Identify rhyme in context.

Materials

- Examples of stories, poetry, and songs that provide rhyme.
- Lists of rhyming words.

Procedures

- Introduce the child to the concept of rhyming words.
- Say a word, and ask the child to say another word that rhymes.
- Provide examples of rhyming and nonrhyming words for the child to identify.
- Read stories and poems together, and allow the child to identify examples of rhyme in context.
- Encourage the child to engage in verbal rhyming games.

Extensions

- Compare rhyming with alliteration, which is the repeated use of an initial sound, not necessarily the identical consonant. For example, Peter Piper picked a peck of pickled peppers or Kangaroos can carry koalas.
- Introduce homophones, words that sound the same but are spelled differently and have different meanings. For example, blew and blue, threw and through, there and their, or two, too, to.

FACT AND FICTION

It is important to introduce young children to nonfiction as well as to fictional picture books. There has been a recent influx of high quality, easy-reading, factual books that couple color photographs of actual objects and events with concise explanations of phenomena. Both boys and girls enjoy factual books as well as stories.

There are different skills required to interpret factual texts and stories. Exposing children to both styles helps lay a foundation for them to become independent readers. They also need to be able to recognize what could actually happen versus what could not happen within a story. For example, *Hot Air Henry* contains accurate factual information about flying hot air balloons, but it is presented in the storyline of a cat flying the balloon—an utter impossibility. Learning how to differentiate between possible and impossible requires guidance.

Prerequisite Skills

- A developing sense of real and imaginary.

Concepts

- Nonfiction books provide factual information.
- Fiction books, whether from the easy or novel sections of the library, are make-believe stories.
- In a library, books are categorized as fiction or nonfiction.

Materials

- Various fiction and nonfiction books.

Procedures

- Before starting the book, discuss whether it is fiction or factual nonfiction.

- Identify clues that help to indicate which type of book you are reading. For example, look for indexes, sub-headings in the text, captions under pictures to indicate nonfiction; look for quotation marks and dialogue, the wording of the title, and the type of illustrations to suggest a storybook.
- Categorize components of the story as being realistic or fanciful.
- Discuss how the author weaves the two together throughout the story.

Extensions

- Introduce basics of Dewey Classification System—not memorizing specific call numbers, but recognizing that materials on the same topic are shelved together.
- Explain how biographies are a kind of nonfiction that provide information about a person's life.
- Discuss the unique characteristics that identify a specific title as belonging to a category, such as science book, history book, geography book, poetry book, fairy tale, or biography.

PUNCTUATION MARKS

Punctuation consists of certain marks in writing and printing that help make the writer's meaning clear. The experienced reader responds to these marks when reading orally by changing characteristics of the voice: a raised pitch of voice indicates a question, increased intensity and volume occur in response to an exclamation point, a drop in pitch accompanied by a pause represents a period. While there are roughly a dozen punctuation marks commonly in use, only the period, question mark, exclamation point, and maybe the idea of quotation marks in conversation, deserve your initial attention. It is important when reading aloud to incorporate the inflection indicated by punctuation so that the child will begin to recognize the connection between printed punctuation marks and the reader's interpretation.

Prerequisite Skills

- Visual discrimination of symbols.
- Recognition that meaning can be indicated by tone of voice and inflection.

Concepts

- Punctuation helps make clear the writer's meaning.
- Different symbols are used for different purposes.
- When reading, pay attention to punctuation as well as words.

Materials

- Books and other written materials.
- Flash cards of punctuation marks.

Procedures

- Use flash cards and have the child match the punctuation marks to those appearing in printed material.
- Demonstrate the effect of punctuation by reading passages aloud. Sometimes read the sentence different ways and ask the child to determine which matches the printed punctuation.
- Have the child suggest the proper punctuation for the sentence verbalized. Develop the child's ability to recognize the distinguishing characteristics of statements, questions, and exclamations.
- Have the child verbalize a sentence, question, or exclamation, given an appropriate prompt.

Extensions

- Introduce the child to Victor Borge's skit on "Phonetic Punctuation."
- Explain additional punctuation marks as appropriate.
- If reading in a language other than English, identify symbols unique to that language.

MAGAZINES AND NEWSPAPERS

Just as adults enjoy receiving subscriptions to periodicals and newspapers, so do children. They look forward to issues of their own periodical arriving regularly in the mail and find their appearance a motivation to read. There are now many periodicals designed for young children. Long-popular publications such as *Cricket* have introduced specialized titles for younger age groups, including *Lady Bug* and *Baby Bug* for preschoolers and toddlers. As children develop interests, you can match periodical subscriptions to them: *Ranger Rick* for an interest in nature, *Sports Illustrated for Kids* for the budding athlete, or *American Girl*, which focuses on topics of interest to young girls, are examples of these. Sharing the *Mini Page* or *Kids* pages that are included in a number of Sunday newspapers introduces the newspaper format.

Prerequisite Skills

- Recognition that information is provided in different formats.

Concepts

- Periodicals or magazines come out regularly, are aimed at a particular audience, and tend to focus on an interest area.
- Newspapers are published more frequently and contain reports of events occurring locally as well as nationally and internationally.
- Publications can be subscribed to and delivered to one's home on a regular basis.

Materials

- Copies of magazines and newspapers.

Procedures

- Look at the periodical publications available at the public library to determine the child's level of interest before ordering a personal subscription.
- Purchase individual copies at the newsstand to assess suitability.
- Share the stories and activities when issues arrive.
- Save back issues for reuse.

Extensions

- Respond to contests or requests for submissions, and write letters to the editor in reaction to specific articles.
- Explore online versions of periodicals.

Chapter 3

Language Arts—Beginning Reading

Beginning reading experiences must strike a balance between the instruction of important word-identification strategies and skills, and frequent interactions with informative and entertaining books. A reason for wanting to read must be established to motivate the learning of skills. When working with a child to develop reading ability, avoid becoming so skill oriented that the meaning and pleasure of reading are lost. At the same time, however, you do need to teach decoding skills and strategies associated with reading so the child can enjoy reading. The child will likely encounter difficulties if you emphasize either approach too much.

Reading is more than the process of phonetically decoding groupings of letters. It is the construction of meaning from printed material. This involves the integration of the reader's background knowledge with new information provided by the text.

Although this segment is called Beginning Reading, it is not the authors' intent to provide a complete instructional guide for teaching reading. Activities suggested are intended to support an individual who is assisting children engaged in teaching themselves to read, or who are engaged in a more formal reading instruction program.

LETTER/SOUND CONNECTIONS

The child who has learned letter names is ready to begin associating speech sounds with written letters. An understanding that there is a limited number of identifiable, individual sounds used in speech and that printed words represent those spoken sounds needs to be developed. Research indicates that this phonemic awareness is the strongest predictor of a child's success in learning to read.

Prerequisite Skills

- Be able to identify letter forms and names.
- Distinguish individual sounds within spoken words.

Concepts

- There is a match between the printed letter and the spoken sound.
- There is a limited number of sounds to work with.
- Knowing the sound/symbol match makes it possible to figure out unknown words.

Materials

- Magnetic letters, flash cards, simple books.
- Chalkboard and chalk or other writing supplies.
- Lists of word families.

Procedures

- It is traditional to begin with consonants, as they are more consistent in their sound/symbol relationship.
- Short vowel sounds follow, as they are primarily encountered in one-syllable words.
- In time, consonant blends such as cr, str, fl, ch and long vowel sounds are introduced.
- Collect objects or pictures of objects that begin with a specific letter sound. Label objects or pictures with the word that matches. Also, attach labels to household objects such as door, bed, table, chair.
- Once the child is familiar with consonant sounds in the initial position, begin to include ending consonants.
- Work with rhyming words.
- Work with word families by exchanging initial consonants to create additional words. For example, at, cat, pat, sat, hat, rat.
- Develop a set of flash cards and individual letter cards to use to practice building words.
- Similarly, use magnetic letters to rearrange and form words.
- Point out words that the child can now read in books.

Extensions

- Add information about multiple sounds for the same letter symbol and more sophisticated phonics rules as needed.

WORD STRUCTURE

A fluent reader begins to associate a single sound with groups of letters that appear frequently in words, which leads to more rapid word identification. Point out suffixes such as -ing, -ed, -full, -ness, and prefixes such as con-, re-, in-, un-. Recognizing the components within compound words such as basketball, raincoat, bedroom, and keyboard gives the child another strategy for decoding.

Prerequisite Skills

- Established sound/symbol connection.

Concepts

- Frequently recurring groups of letters are recognized as a unit.
- Recognizing these groups is a strategy for decoding unfamiliar words.
- Compound words are a combination of individual words.
- Prefixes and suffixes are added to root words.

Materials

- Lists of letter groups that correspond to a sound, such as -tion, -ough, -oon, -ight.
- Lists of compound words.
- Lists of commonly used prefixes and suffixes.

Procedures

- When sharing stories, look for examples that fit patterns.
- Analyze and discuss the words.
- Play word games that focus on the structural components of words.
- Create compound words, change form by adding suffixes, or make a list of words that end in -ful, -ly, -ing, and the like.
- Encourage the child to apply structural clues when decoding unfamiliar words.

Extensions

- Identifying words within words does not always provide phonetic clues, but it is interesting and provides practice in word recognition: for example, *am* in the middle of *name*, in which the short "a" of *am* becomes long with the addition of the final "e" in *name*.
- Explore syllabification rules for dividing words.
- Compare compound words in which the meaning reflects the component words, to those that produce a whole new meaning, for example, raincoat, campfire, bedroom to buttercup, footlocker, or grapefruit.
- Investigate how prefixes and suffixes influence the meaning of words.

SIGHT WORDS

Beginning readers recognize very few words at sight. It is only with repeated exposure that sight vocabulary is developed. The time spent learning to read these words produces a major payoff, since approximately one hundred words comprise 50 percent of all words adult readers encounter. Many of these words need to be learned by sight because they are not phonetically regular. For example, when the child attempts to apply phonetic generalizations, the word *to* should rhyme with *go* and *said* should rhyme with *paid*. The process of slowly analyzing individual words when reading diverts memory and attention that is needed to comprehend the material being read. The development of a sight vocabulary helps reduce the struggle.

Prerequisite Skills

- Recognition that words are groups of letters.

Concepts

- Sight vocabulary allows the recognition of total words without analyzing component letters and sounds.
- Learning to recognize the hundred or so basic sight words builds reading fluency.
- There are exceptions to phonic generalizations.

Materials

- List of basic sight words.
- Flash card set of these words.
- Controlled vocabulary stories that provide practice with these frequently used words.

Procedures

- Practice recognizing these words in gamelike formats, such as matching activities, picking out words in response to verbal prompts, finding examples of the words in print material.
- Have child create sentences using the flash-card words.
- Have child point out examples of sight words in the text of stories being read to them.
- Have child practice writing these words.

Extensions

- Label objects around the child's environment to provide additional opportunity to see words in print.

USING PICTURE AND CONTEXT CLUES

All readers use context clues to help with unfamiliar words and meanings. The beginning reader depends on the use of picture clues for assistance with words, then, as experience increases, begins to use semantic or meaning clues. There are probable words associated with any topic—for example, winter suggests words like snow, wind, ice, sled, mittens, boots, cold. When encountering an unfamiliar word, an initial guess might be one of these expected words. Word order also provides clues in that the structure of the sentence indicates the type of word needed to make sense—an action, a description, or a naming word fits into particular contexts. Being alert to these clues helps to determine an accurate match between the pronunciation arrived at from phonetic analysis and meaning derived from the context. Building the habit of cross-checking helps assure accurate word choice.

Prerequisite Skills

- The ability to interpret simple still pictures.
- An established sense of sentence structure.
- A feeling for the functions of words—action, descriptive, or naming words.
- A basic vocabulary and the ability to recognize words related to a given topic.

Concepts

- Pictures on the page provide clues to suggest a possible word when faced with unfamiliar text.
- The context of the sentence helps suggest a possible word when the child is faced with unfamiliar text.
- Sentence structure provides clues to suggest a possible word in an unfamiliar text.

Materials

- Variety of books to share and to begin reading independently.

Procedures

- Provide opportunities for the child to practice using picture and context clues during shared reading.
- Model these behaviors for the child by talking through the process. Ask the child to supply the next word in

situations where a connection can be made between picture or context clues and an appropriate word.

- When the child becomes stuck and requests help, suggest using a picture clue or context strategy to determine the needed word.

Extensions

- As the child becomes a more independent reader, encourage the child to share instances when an attempt to apply these strategies is made.

VOCABULARY ENRICHMENT

The larger the spoken vocabulary, the easier it is for the child to recognize the words being decoded. Take advantage of every opportunity to expand a child's vocabulary. The simplest approach is to talk with the child and use vocabulary appropriate for the subject without substituting simplified words when providing explanations or definitions. You can also use experiences in the neighborhood, television viewing, and shared reading to introduce new vocabulary. Nurturing an interest in words and vocabulary development cannot begin too early.

Prerequisite Skills

- The child responds to the caregiver's demonstrated interest in vocabulary development.

Concepts

- Learning new words is enjoyable.
- Using the right word in the right place is important for communication.
- There is specialized vocabulary related to most activities.
- To derive meaning from reading, the word has to be in one's vocabulary.

Materials

- Thesaurus, dictionary.
- Notebook for writing down new words.
- Sources for developing vocabulary such as concrete experiences, books, videos, content-related CDs, interactions with others.

Procedures

- When talking with the child, verify that the child understands the vocabulary you have used.
- When sharing books, verify the child's comprehension as you go along.
- Encourage the child to ask for explanations of words and occurrences not understood.
- Help the child maintain a list of these new words to learn.
- Listen to the child's talk, and correct errors in word usage. Explain the misuse of the word.
- Nurture an interest in words related to a topic of interest to the child. For example, when the child dis-

covers space, dinosaurs, underwater habitats, or develops an interest in a sport, encourage vocabulary development related to the activity.

Extensions

- Use calendars that present a word of the day or thematic vocabulary.
- Pick a topic—such as food, clothes, weather, frogs—and ask the child to generate a list of words or phrases that start with each letter of the alphabet. Sometimes it is necessary to be creative with the wording to achieve a needed initial letter; for example, in a frog alphabet the word *eyes* could be used for the letter "e," and adding descriptive words could supply suitable words for the letter "b," such as *big, bulgy eyes*.
- If you want, you can help the child fill in gaps in such an alphabet activity by together consulting dictionaries or indexes in books on the topic. Remember that it is not always necessary to create an entry for every letter if by doing so the fun element is lost. Also, multiple entries can be recorded for a given letter. Using clothes as a topic, the child might think shirt, skirt, shoes, shorts, sweater, socks for the letter "s" but struggle to think of quilted jacket or vest for the more challenging letters "q" and "v."

Chapter 4

Language Arts—Beginning Writing

Children's early writing will not match standards for adult writing. Children first write by drawing. They "read" their drawings, recalling events to tell a story. Their concept of writing becomes visible when they begin to scribble, which resembles writing in spacing and alignment. The next step is probably recognizing that one's name is made up of letters and the exploration of writing actual letters in random combinations. At this stage of development, it is not unusual for the child to reverse letters and numbers when forming them. In time, the child uses invented spelling to convey sound/symbol relationships once that concept is learned. The development of writing is enhanced when a child has access to pencils, crayons, markers, and paper, or has chalk and a chalkboard. Picking out letters on a computer keyboard can also motivate an interest in writing.

DRAWING AS COMMUNICATION

Using drawings to communicate permits the child to share ideas in a written format: one can name things, describe actions, sequence events, and express opinions. Children's pictures contain objects (tree, dog, house, person, bike), show actions (riding a bicycle, playing catch, walking on the beach), and illustrate feelings (facial expressions, use of color, placement of characters on the page). It is essential that the adult realize that the picture is a form of communication and listen to the child describe its message. Take care not to focus on evaluating the drawing in terms of its artistic qualities at the expense of sharing the message being communicated to avoid inhibiting the child's future attempts.

Prerequisite Skills

- Eye/hand coordination sufficient to control drawing materials.
- The desire to express thoughts and feelings.

Concepts

- Drawings can represent objects, events, and actions.
- Drawings can communicate messages.
- Drawings can tell stories.

Materials

- Paper, markers, crayons, pencils.
- Rather than use new paper, collect sheets already used on one side.

Procedures

- Provide an environment that includes markers, paper, and a surface to work on.
- Encourage sharing of the message communicated by the child's drawings.
- Provide a place to display the child's drawings.

Extensions

- Add any text dictated by the child.
- When discussing the drawing with the child, ask questions to solicit descriptions of what may have happened before or after the event pictured.

SCRIBBLING

At the scribbling stage, the child begins to incorporate conventions of standard writing: the left-to-right progression, marks that are spaced and aligned to give the impression of words. One can see more fine-muscle control of the pencil or marker. The marks are intended as writing even though they do not contain conventionally formed letters. The child brings meaning to these marks when "reading" them back to someone.

Prerequisite Skills

- Ability to hold markers, pencils, crayons.
- Ability to control the paper while moving the markers.
- The desire to communicate.

Concepts

- Words are groups of symbols.
- Groups of symbols have meaning.
- What one can say can be written.

Materials

- Assorted markers and paper supplies.

Procedures

- Give the child materials and a place to write.
- Share with the child samples of hand-written messages and notes or lists you use.
- Give the child your attention when he or she wants to share or discuss what their writing means to them.

Extensions

- Keep magnetic letters on the refrigerator to raise awareness.
- Begin to model the proper formation of letters when writing the child's name or other words.
- Point out examples of letters the child can recognize in other contexts, such as advertisements, billboards, store signs, license plates, etc.

DICTATING WRITING

To facilitate the child's early attempts to communicate in writing, offer to write down for them what they want to say. Add a caption to a picture they draw. Write down a passage the child dictates and illustrates later. Write a letter to send to Grandma or Santa or address the envelope to send a child-made card. Providing this type of personal application of the use of written communication helps the child develop a need to write independently.

Prerequisite Skills

- Recognition that what can be said can be written.

Concepts

- Only standardized symbols in recognizable sequences convey meaning to others.
- If you cannot do it yourself, you can get someone else to do it for you.
- Written information can be saved and shared.

Materials

- Writing or drawing paper and markers.
- Envelopes and stamps.

Procedures

- Encourage the child to dictate statements, stories, or letters.
- Write them down and send, share, or display products.

Extensions

- Pair the child's scribbling or invented spelling attempts with the standard version.
- Use computer programs that allow the child to record their voice telling what the picture/text they created is meant to say.

INVENTED SPELLING

Children create their own spellings for words when they do not know conventional spelling. A single letter may represent an entire word or syllable, and they may only use beginning and ending consonants at first. For example, BT might mean bat, BK might be used for back or bike. As children learn to differentiate sounds, they include more letters, with vowels coming last. The value of invented spelling use is that the child is not limited to writing only the words they know how to spell correctly. They can use their verbal vocabulary and focus on the content of what they want to communicate. They do not have to write "big dog" when they really want to write "huge ferocious beast." The focus should be on the quality of the content being communicated. Editing is a process that follows getting ideas recorded and should not become an obstacle to expression.

Prerequisite Skills

- Recognition of letters.
- Begin to match a sound with the symbols that are used to represent it.

Materials

- Writing materials including crayons, pencils, pens, paper, or computer keyboard.

Concepts

- Communication depends on the common interpretation of symbols.
- One's ideas are worth communicating.
- One's use of nonconventional spelling will be replaced as learning increases.

Procedures

- Encourage the child to write frequently.
- Encourage the child to sound out words rather than always requesting the authentic spelling.
- Show the child how much you can read of what is written in the child's invented spelling.

Extensions

- Introduce the steps in the writing process: prewriting, writing, revision, editing, sharing.
- Select a sample of the child's writing to work through the steps in the process. Not everything the child writes should be taken through the entire process.

Chapter 5

Visual

Children need to be taught how to interpret pictures and other visual formats. People often assume that children learn to read picture clues intuitively. This may be true for the lower end of the continuum of visual literacy skills such as being able to name objects in an illustration. The higher level skills—such as being able to predict what will happen next or what happened before the event in the picture, or being able to understand such special effects as flashbacks or point of view as shown by camera angles— require more direct teaching. Talking with children about the illustrations in picture books, calendars, or discussing their understanding of movies and television shows will guide them in developing important visual literacy skills.

READING STILL PICTURES

As with reading text there are distinct skills associated with the ability to read pictures. One's experiences and background knowledge influence the meaning that is obtained. With practice, one can enhance the meaning obtained.

When you give the child strategies for interpreting visual representations, you increase the likelihood of accurate comprehension.

Prerequisite Skills

• The ability to differentiate visual representations.

Concepts

• Pictures represent real objects.
• Pictures provide information.
• Pictures give us clues to time and place.
• Pictures evoke emotions.

Materials

• Wide variety of pictures.

Procedures

• While sharing stories or other visuals, have the child point to and name objects shown.
• Introduce questions that ask the child to tell you what is happening in the picture.
• Ask the child to predict what might have happened before and/or after the event shown in the picture. Try to elicit multiple predictions. Reassure that there is no absolutely correct response, but that predictions should be based on information provided by the picture. Have the child identify the most reasonable prediction and give some reasons.

- Direct the child to make inferences that can be supported by looking at the picture, finding clues that suggest the season, geographic location, time of day, whether the situation is real or imagined, and whether it represents the present, past, or future.

Extensions

- Go to art museums and interpret art works.
- Draw your own pictures and describe the intended message.
- Using wordless books, create stories to accompany the illustrations.
- Predict the story in new picture books by looking at the pictures. Verify the prediction by reading the author's story.

INTERPRETING ICON SIGNS

As a response to language barriers there is a series of standardized graphic representations that are used internationally. Such signage uses visual symbols to represent universal services and to indicate where the service can be obtained. Children need to develop an awareness of this type of visual communication—often a blue-and-white sign. Food services are indicated by a knife and fork, lodging by a bed, fuel by a gas pump, restrooms by male and female characters, library by a letter L representing a person holding a book, a hospital by a capital H, airport by a plane, train stations by a train, and so on. The use of icons as a means of communication continues to expand.

Prerequisite Skills

- The ability to differentiate visual symbols.
- Understand that visuals provide information.

Concepts

- There is a connection between specific visuals and their meaning.
- The symbol is instantly and universally recognizable.

Materials

- Photographs, hand drawings, the signs themselves to illustrate various icons and their uses.

Procedures

- Point out examples of icons as encountered throughout the community—hospital, library, metro, school crossing, railroad, stop sign and so forth.
- Look for examples of icons in storybooks, newspaper copy, television shows or movies.

Extensions

- Learn international road signs.
- Locate the icons on computer components and other electronic equipment that facilitate assembly and use.
- Find examples of signs that denote hiking trails (for example, the Appalachian trail), picnic grounds, roadside tables, campgrounds, metro, trailer parks, tele-

phones, and numerous other recreational and service application signs.

- Look for commercial use of icons and trademarks— the Golden Arches of McDonald's, KFC for Kentucky Fried Chicken, Pillsbury's Doughboy, sports team logos, clothing labels, automobile emblems—the examples abound.
- Discover symbols that identify a specific geographic location such as the Eiffel Tower in Paris, Big Ben in London, the Statue of Liberty in New York, koala bears for Australia, or an Alphorn for Switzerland.

BASIC ART CONCEPTS

Fundamental elements in art include color, line, shape, and perspective, and all are within the grasp of the child. A person who understands these concepts and the related vocabulary can have meaningful discussions of pictures. These same understandings are beneficial to the child in creating art projects or enjoying the art work of others.

Prerequisite Skills

- Sufficient attention span to focus on a visual for a period of time.

Concepts

- Each color has a term to identify it.
- Relationship between primary and secondary colors.
- Lines are boundaries between areas and vary in width and length.

- The basic shapes are square, rectangle, triangle, and circle.
- Perspective depicts depth and/or distance.

Materials

- Variety of art materials to use.
- Examples of art work which demonstrate the concepts: Illustrations in children's books, museum reproductions, prints, or art originals.

Procedures

- Develop color recognition by naming the colors of objects.
- Develop shape recognition by matching name of shape with examples using pattern blocks, cutouts, and eventually real objects.
- Provide experiences in creating lines of different lengths and widths, curved and straight. Draw line pictures creating recognizable objects.
- Examine pictures and focus the child's attention on identifying the use and effect of colors, shapes, and lines in the picture.
- Expand your discussion to explain the effect of perspective, repetition, light and shadow, and other special effects.

Extensions

- Expand concept of color to include shades and tints and the names of less familiar colors.

- Expand the concept of shapes to include a variety of polygons and their names.
- Introduce concept of optical illusions and techniques such as pointillism or cubism.
- Introduce specific artists connected with a specific style.

SEQUENCING

Sequencing is a method that demonstrates comprehension of a process. Many processes in nature are sequential: for example, the seasons, water cycle, life cycle, food chain, day and night. Daily life generally follows a sequence. The child comes to recognize these familiar sequences and needs to be guided in transferring this process to help organize less familiar material. The child must begin to recognize clues that establish position within a sequence, and learn when the sequence is optional or fixed. For example, history follows a fixed chronological sequence but an author has flexibility in sequencing events when creating a story. A visually literate person is able to interpret pictures and sequence them in a logical order that communicates their message. In this day and age of multimedia productions, sequencing and interpreting a sequence of visuals is a vital skill.

Prerequisite Skills

- An emerging sense of beginning, middle, and end.
- The ability to recognize clues in pictures that provide context needed for sequencing.

Concepts

- There are various patterns for sequencing, such as size or color, or chronological, alphabetical, and developmental orders.
- Visuals contain clues that provide guidance in determining a sequence.
- Some sets of visuals may be sequenced in a variety of ways; for others, there may be only one acceptable sequence.

Materials

- Visuals that relate to each other in some way.
- Comics cut apart for resequencing.
- Sets of seemingly unrelated visuals.

Procedures

- Ask the child to sequence a set of pictures and to explain the reasons for placement in the sequence.
- Have a group of children reach consensus as to an appropriate sequence for a given set of pictures and give their reasoning behind suggested picture placement.
- Direct the child to create visuals representing procedural activities such as getting dressed or making a sandwich. Evaluate the finished sequence of pictures for accuracy and any omission of important steps.
- Resequence comic-strip frames.

Extensions

- Assemble a sequence with a missing segment. Ask the child to fill in the missing piece.
- Use a commercial computer program designed to practice sequencing of visuals.

CATEGORIZING

Categorizing is a useful strategy for organizing a collection of items or data. The same items can be regrouped using different attributes for determining membership in a group. This thought strategy has broad applications and should be developed in every child. Sorting and grouping items is instinctual; what needs guidance is the ability to see possibilities for regrouping in other ways. This flexibility in thinking generates new insights and leads to problem solving. Many times, it is a visual attribute that is the basis for grouping.

Prerequisite Skills

- The ability to recognize differences in color, size, shape, function.
- The recognition of commonalities among items.

Concepts

- Membership in a group is based on a shared or common attribute.
- The same items can be regrouped in a number of ways depending upon the attribute that defines membership in the group.
- Items have multiple attributes.

Materials

- Wide variety of concrete items or visuals to be categorized.
- List of visual attributes that could be used for categorizing.

Procedures

- Early experiences can focus on a limited number of items to categorize, using obvious attributes such as color, shape, or size to form the groups.
- As the child's skill increases, introduce more subtle or sophisticated attributes to look for. Offer the child a collection of pictures and a prompt related to the season of year, number of objects in a picture, geographic location (rural or urban), work or play, or the like.
- The next step is for the child to determine the groupings and explain the attributes used to make the groups. The same set of visuals could be given to multiple children with varying results. Discuss the explanations given for making groups and assigning membership.

Extensions

- Introduce the concept of a Venn diagram as a format for categorizing. Objects with shared attributes are placed in the overlap while objects with just one of the attributes are placed in the outer areas of the appropriate circle. Items with neither attribute are placed outside the circles.

- Using pictures from catalogs, old calendars, or magazines, create thematic collages. Themes can be related to units of study (animals, plants, foods, family, holidays), initial consonant sounds (things starting with the letter "b," "s," "m"), or the child's "self-portrait" of items depicting life experiences and interests.

INTERPRETING MOTION PICTURES

Other skills are required to interpret motion media accurately. The director manipulates the audience through the integration of special effects, camera angles, time lapse, flashbacks, and animation. The untrained viewer can misinterpret images when the use of these effects is not recognized. Recognition of these techniques does not diminish the enjoyment of the film, but it does allow the viewer to retain a sense of reality. The young viewer needs to be introduced to these techniques so as not to be misled. Without appropriate intervention, young children try to emulate what they see in movies and on TV. The results can range from disappointment to disaster. Advertising is designed to make the product look irresistible; in reality, the product frequently disappoints by not living up to expectations. A child's attempt to replicate what they see happening in cartoons, where there is virtually no physical injury to the cartoon characters, can result in a medical emergency for the child. Time spent in shared viewing and discussion helps develop the child's visual literacy.

Prerequisite Skills

- Ability to independently turn on TVs and VCRs, leading to opportunities for unsupervised viewing.

Concepts

- Real and make-believe are not the same and are not interchangeable.
- The camera can be manipulated to produce special effects that alter the reality of time and space.
- Camera angles are used to portray subtle messages of power, value, and point of view.
- Body language is evident in motion sequences.
- Seeing is not necessarily believing.

Materials

- Samples of motion media.

Procedures

- Preview a film and identify segments that illustrate the concepts.
- Provide time for shared viewing and discussion based on this.
- Assess the child's ability to accurately interpret the segment.
- Be alert during shared viewing of normal TV programming for examples to discuss with the child. Listen to the child's interpretation of what was seen and correct misconceptions expressed by the child.
- Ask questions that probe for misconceptions that may

not have been expressed in order to discuss and correct them.

Extensions

- Record segments with a video camera to demonstrate the manipulative power of film. When children create video productions and recognize the fake reality they have created, they become more critical viewers of commercial TV programs.
- Examine commercials to identify examples of audience manipulation. For example, close-up shots make an item look bigger; pairing an item with accessories or something desirable that does not come with it when it is purchased; and small-print disclaimers that flash by unnoticed by a nonreader.

VISUAL/SPATIAL RELATIONSHIPS

The ability to recognize and manipulate visual/spatial relationships is one characteristic evaluated when screening young children for giftedness. Visual techniques such as cross-sections and cutaways present three-dimensional information on the flat pages of a book, and their interpretation requires the ability to comprehend spatial relationships. CD-ROMs that incorporate motion to provide these perspectives demonstrate nicely the peeling away of layers, which helps visualization. You can help children develop the ability to recognize patterns, identify a missing piece, recognize the relationship between the position of the viewer and what can be seen, and how this is altered when the position of the viewer is changed.

Prerequisite Skills

- Comprehension of terms such as top, bottom, right, left, inside, outside, turn around, rotate.

Concepts

- There is a relationship between part and whole.
- The specific manipulation of an object has a resulting effect.
- Mental imaging and visualization play a role in creating different perspectives.
- Cutaways, cross-sections, and 3–D perspective are all spatial techniques.
- Patterns are part of visual/spatial relationships.

Materials

- Jigsaw puzzles.
- Books of visual/spatial puzzles.
- Books containing cut-away and cross-section illustrations.

Procedures

- Work with the child on age-appropriate jigsaw puzzles. Help recognize and apply strategies for fitting pieces together: continuation of line or color, relationship of the outline of the piece and the shape of the space, turning a piece around, and so forth.
- Create puzzles from wrapping paper or wallpaper samples. Cut a small section out of each paper sample.

Ask the child to fill in the missing sections with the cutouts matching patterns and backgrounds.

- Discuss illustrations in books to verify the child's understanding of visual techniques. Ask questions such as: what would you see if you were standing in a particular location relative to the illustration, where is something in relation to something else, where is the source of light, what would you see if you walked from one place to another within the illustration.

- Read a passage and ask the child to draw a picture that shows the relationships described in the passage. Review why the child put the objects where they did in the drawing. Reread the passage following the drawing to verify accuracy of understanding.

- Use activity books to locate examples of visual/spatial puzzles, such as hidden pictures, mazes, or finding matching items.

Extensions

- Share *Where's Waldo?*–type books.
- Explore time-lapse, slow-motion, microscopic footage related to scientific topics.

Chapter 6

Math

An important concept for children to understand is that mathematics is not just something to study in school but rather something you use daily in life. For this reason it is essential that early experiences with math concepts such as counting, measuring, and calculating be set in the context of routine, daily activities. Counting buttons while dressing a toddler, counting toys while cleaning up after playtime, counting stairs while going up or down takes no more time than doing the activity without counting. Pointing out examples of numbers on objects around the house, car, classroom, or in printed sources such as books, magazines, maps, or the telephone book builds an awareness of numbers. Verbalizing examples of how you apply math concepts during everyday tasks such as shopping, cooking, and doing the laundry, counting, calculating or measuring focuses awareness on numbers and their value. Awareness of numbers and how important people find them to be in their lives, motivates young children to discover their properties and begin to want to control them independently. Playing various board games and card games provides practice in basic math skills.

NUMBER CONCEPT

Before being asked to manipulate numbers, the child needs to develop the concept of a numeric quantity and be able to match it with the appropriate written symbol—the symbol "1" with a single item, the symbol "2" with two items, and so on. This is a different skill from being able to count sequentially, which is also essential. Just because the child can identify numbers of items in specific settings does not mean that the concept has been internalized to allow transfer to all situations.

Prerequisite Skills

- Be able to count
- Can identify numbers out of sequence and begin to associate the symbol with the concept.
- Pick out like items from a set of mixed items.

Concepts

- Numeric quantities are represented by numbers.
- A set is a group of items. The items may be the same or assorted; e.g., a set of placemats that are alike or a set of toys that includes a truck, a ball, a soldier, an animal.

Materials

- No specific items are required. Pictures of items, as well as the items themselves, can be used. For example, a mail-order catalog that has pictures of different numbers of items such as belts, shoes, socks, flowers, tools, or toys can be cut up to provide visuals to match with numbers. Such manipulatives are inexpensive and consumable and are easily replaced. They can be selected to fit the current interest of the child—sports, toys, tools, clothes, whatever.

- Collections of readily available inexpensive items such as bottle caps, clothespins, Popsicle sticks, buttons, pebbles, small toys, or commercially made counters also provide manipulatives for these activities.

Procedures

- Show a numerical symbol. Ask the child to create a set of items that matches the symbol. This can be done in a variety of formats. The number can be written on a piece of paper; the child can place the correct number of items, or pictured items, on the paper. Items can be reused or pasted in place.
- A circle of yarn, a hula hoop, or a jump rope laid in a circle on the floor provides a boundary for the child to place objects inside and permits the child to move about physically while creating sets.
- Using laminated posters or cards and water-soluble markers, the child can circle or mark the appropriate number of items. The card can be wiped clean and re-used. Chalk boards offer another possibility.
- Ask the child to hold up the correct number of fingers to match the number that is said.
- Prompt the child with a set of items and ask the child to give the numeric symbol. Responses can be oral or written.

- Use dice or playing cards to establish recognition of patterns traditionally used to represent numbers.

Extensions

- Verify mastery of the concepts by encouraging the child to successfully complete tasks such as setting the table or locating a specific number of requested items.
- Once the child has mastered the basic concepts of "1," "2," "3," and so forth, introduce first, second, third, and so on.
- Once the child has the concept of "10," introduce place value and the patterning for teens, twenties, thirties, forties, and onward.
- Introduce the concept of skip-counting—counting by 2s, 5s, 10s, and the like. Also introduce counting backwards.

MEASUREMENT

Measurement is one of the oldest skills. Measurement is needed to answer frequently asked questions such as "how many," "how much," "how long," or "how far." Every measurement involves two things: a number and a unit. Standard units of measure provide consistency and uniformity among peoples, but the concept of measurement can employ nonstandard units such as the child's length of a shoe, paper clips, favorite object, or cereal box. Once the child understands the basic concept of using a unit of measurement, then introduce traditional units such as feet, yards, miles, ounces, pounds, cups, pints, gallons, minutes, hours, and the like.

The vocabulary of measurement is not interchangeable. Specific terms relate to weight, time, speed, length, solids, liquids, area, and volume, with specialized terms applying to measurement of areas such as sound, electricity, or gems. It is important to establish the habit of labeling the measurement with the unit used. The number "six" alone could refer to anything from mosquito bites to miles and becomes meaningful only by labeling. As with anything else, talking about one's actions while measuring helps raise the child's awareness and motivates learning.

Prerequisite Skills

- The ability to count and sequence numbers.
- The concept of using a measurement tool accurately, of determining the proper placement of the tool when it must be reused as in linear measure.

Concepts

- Measurement permits comparison of items.
- The same unit of measure must be used when making comparisons or establishing relationships.
- Any unit can be used to measure for personal use, but in order to have meaning for someone else, standard units of measure must be used.
- The number measured must be labeled with the name of the unit used in order to be meaningful.

Materials

- A variety of standard measuring tools, including rulers, yardsticks, tape measures; balances and scales; cups, liters, pints, quarts, gallons.
- Nonstandard units of measure such as paper clips, box, chalkboard eraser, various sized plastic and paper containers (jars, bottles); unopened canned or packaged goods.
- An assortment of things to "measure."

Procedures

- Ask child to measure by footlengths the distance across a room or from point A to B; or figured out how many teddy bears long a bed is; or how many spoonfuls of cereal fill a dish; or how many cereal boxes fit across the table.
- If you have access to a balance scale, begin establishing the concept of equal weight, heavier than, and lighter than. When comparing the weights of individual assorted items, the unit of measure on the other side of the balance scale needs to be the same. Crayons, pencils, paper clips, counters, checkers, clothespins, bolts, washers, or standard weights, if they are available, may be used.
- Give the child containers of various shapes and sizes to play with in the bathtub or wading pool. Encourage the child to discover relationships between shape and volume—for example, the tall, thin container holds the same as a short, fat one. Point out equation relationships—such as three small containers are needed to fill one large one. Figure out together the

consistency factor—that every time the process is carried out, the results are the same.
- Once the principles are acquired using nonstandard units of measure, start to bring in standard units of measure in a more formal setting. Show how to use rulers, yardsticks, and tape measures for lengths of items; ounces and pounds for weight; and teaspoons, cups, pints, quarts, and gallons for liquid. Measure the length of pieces of furniture, the hallway, jacket sleeves, pieces of string or tape (laid down on the floor or table); the width of the door or a book; the height of chairs, tables, or people. Using a bathroom scale, measure the weight in pounds of various objects and people. While cooking, involve the child in measuring activities using cups, teaspoons, and tablespoons.

Extensions

- Incorporate vocabulary terms such as longer, shorter, lighter, heavier, more, less, louder, softer.
- When appropriate, introduce specialized measurement terms such as wattage of lightbulbs; metric units; sizes of batteries, clothing, knitting needles, tires; and air pressure in tires and barometers.

TELLING TIME

Connecting time on the clock to events in the daily routine is a meaningful way to introduce the concept of time. Meals, waking up, bedtime, favorite TV programs, someone coming home from or leaving for work, are all daily events that the child anticipates, or at least recognizes, and can learn to associate with specific numbers or hand positions on the clock. The child needs to be comfortable reading both digital and analog types of clocks. In connection with learning to interpret the meaning of the numbers (and/or hands) on a clock, the concepts of being on time, early, and late need to be established. The importance of being on time, as well as the impact of being early or late, needs to be learned. The process of internalizing how long an hour is, or exactly when last week or next year—or even tomorrow—occurs takes much longer to develop than learning to tell time by the clock.

Prerequisite Skills

- Recognizes numbers.
- Can differentiate long and short hands on the clock face.
- Counts by fives.
- Comprehends before and after.

Concepts

- Units of time break down into hours, minutes, seconds.
- A.M. and P.M. divide the hours of the day.

Materials

- Digital and analog clocks.

Procedures

- Make connections for the child between daily events and the time on the clock. Focus on hours and half hours.
- Next, introduce minutes. Depending on which kind of clock being used, break the hour into units of five minutes (analog) or one minute (digital). Practice by periodically asking the child to tell you what time it is, or tell the child what will happen at a given time: "You may have a cookie at 3:15," or "You may turn the TV on at 4:30."
- The next step is the concept of duration of time: "We'll leave in ten minutes," "You may play with Johnny for a half-hour," "You may use the computer in an hour," or "I'll read you a story at bedtime (or at 7:20)." Discuss with the child the link between the numbers on the clock and the promise made.

Extensions

- As concepts develop, introduce the meaning of A.M. and P.M. and noon and midnight.
- Give the child the chance to recount events of the day in appropriate sequence.
- Use the concepts of "today," "tomorrow," and "yesterday" accurately.
- Have the child help reset clocks after power outages and at seasonal adjustments for daylight saving time.
- Differences in time zones can be explained in reference to where family and friends live, or travel plans.
- Learn to read clocks and watches that use alternate symbols on their faces: Roman numerals, just dots or

lines without numbers to mark some of the hours, graphic representations of hobbies or interests (spider web, Mickey Mouse, train on track, etc.).

CALENDARS

Another tool for telling time is the calendar. A child who has the sense of weeks, months, and years has a foundation for understanding the chronology of historical events. Although young children do not have an accurate sense of long periods of time such as decades and centuries, they can comprehend annual events such as birthdays, holidays, and seasons. Days of the week and months of the year are terms the child needs to become familiar with. The relationships between days, weeks, months, and years need to be learned. Also, various formats of the standard calendar need to be interpreted. While all calendars contain the same information, it is not always arranged using the same format. The child needs to develop the flexibility to make meaning of the various arrangements.

Prerequisite Skills

- Top-to-bottom and left-to-right sequencing.
- Recognize the names and abbreviations for the months of the year and days of the week.
- Sequence of the days of the week.

Concepts

- There are patterns of days and weeks within a month.
- There is a pattern of months within the year.

- Months have varying number of days, therefore the first of the month falls on different days.
- Develop meaning of the terms "yesterday" and "tomorrow."
- Apply ordinal numbers to the days and weeks of the month—first, second, third, fourth, and so on. Sometimes there is a fifth and always a last.
- Apply the correct interpretation of the term "next." When "next Wednesday" comes depends on what the current day is.

Materials

- Various types of calendars.

Procedures

- Give the child a personal calendar. Together, identify special days with stickers or markings. Each day talk about which day it is, and check off the passing of another day. Talk about which day is "tomorrow" and which is "yesterday." Name the month and identify the date as a part of a daily routine.
- Play games with the child having them point to a specific place on the calendar identified by day or date. Expand this to include prompts such as the "third Tuesday" or the "next Wednesday after the 12th."
- For months, separate the pages of a calendar and have the child resequence them. Don't always start with January; start with the child's birth month or the school year to ensure total understanding of the sequence.

Extensions

- Show the child some esoteric calendars, such as those having multiple years, manipulative pieces, or thematic approaches.
- Talk about leap year and its effect on the calendar.
- Explore the pattern of repetition. How many years before a calendar repeats exactly?
- Introduce historical calendars developed by other civilizations.
- Explore how dates are determined for holidays and feasts that occur on different dates year-to-year. Examples are Chinese New Year, Rosh Hashanah, Easter, Mother's Day, Labor Day, and Thanksgiving, as opposed to Halloween, Christmas, Independence Day, Valentine's Day, and April Fool's Day, all of which always occur on the same date year-to-year.

MONEY

Handling money is a lifelong need. It is important to introduce young children to the vocabulary and processes of handling money. They will best learn how to identify various coins and bills and their value by actually buying, receiving change, and saving. Supervised practice builds the competence for making independent transactions, so take advantage of the opportunities for discussing the relationships between the cash register total, the money given the clerk, and the change returned. An allowance allows for decision-making practice related to immediate spending or saving for an item of greater worth. Many banks offer Young Savers Clubs, with special services to encourage maintaining a savings account.

Prerequisite Skills

- The ability to recognize differences in the appearance of coins.
- The ability to count by fives and tens.
- Grasp of the connection between the use of money and the making of purchases.

Concepts

- There are relationships between specific coins and bills.
- Change is the difference between purchase price and money tendered.
- One needs to wait for and verify the accuracy of change given.

Materials

- Assorted coins and bills (either play or real).
- Items to "play store" with to role play the purchasing process.

Procedures

- Manipulate play or real money to demonstrate relationships among coins.
- Ask the child to demonstrate different combinations that equal a nickel, dime, quarter, and a dollar. Make certain the child associates the sense of value rather than of size with the coin.
- Role play purchasing single items by using the coins or bills to equal the exact cost. Limit initial experiences to values equaling a dollar or less.

- Role play purchasing single items in which the child pays with a dollar and needs to determine the change.
- Role play purchasing multiple items so that the concept of totaling the cost is introduced.
- As the child masters the skills, introduce the use of larger denomination bills.
- Involve the child in actual, supervised purchasing.

Extensions

- Discuss delayed versus immediate gratification as they relate to spending and saving.
- Calculate sales tax and explain its purpose.
- Expose the child to foreign currency and its value relative to the dollar.
- Compare the relative value of items. Is the item worth its price?
- Determine the best buy.
- Discuss added costs of buying on credit.
- Open a savings account for the child.

BASIC CALCULATIONS

Although it is important for the child to learn basic facts, it is equally important to build an understanding of the concepts of addition and subtraction. It is critical to provide many experiences with real objects before moving to paper and pencil calculations. The manipulation of concrete objects demonstrates the child's understanding that addition is the total of two or more groups and subtraction is the difference between the total and a part. Merely parroting facts does not exhibit understanding. This type of reasoning is prerequisite to use of a calculator. Unless mathematical processes are understood, a calculator is useless. Additional concepts to develop include equality, greater than and less than, and place value. Mathematical growth requires conceptual development as well as recall of basic facts.

Prerequisite Skills

- Concept of numbers.
- Ability to write numbers.

Concepts

- Establish the concept of a number line.
- Identify the relationship between numbers as being greater than or less than each other.
- Addition is the totaling of sets of items.
- Subtraction is finding the difference between sets.
- Apply regrouping processes as required by place value.

Materials

- A variety of small objects to manipulate (checkers, toothpicks, bottle caps, pennies, etc.).
- Rulers and yardsticks for use as numberlines.

Procedures

- Have the child combine various sets of objects to determine the total. Start with combinations of numbers totaling five or less, and direct the child to make as many combinations as possible to equal numbers up to five. Don't overlook zero.

- Once competence is developed at this level, work on combinations that total up to ten.
- Encourage the discovery of the relationship between addition and subtraction by changing the wording of your prompt. After the child has manipulated sets of 2 and 3 to equal 5, have them take 2 away from 5 and discover that 3 are left. Use the vocabulary of finding the "sum" or "total" for addition and "difference" for subtraction.
- Going beyond ten requires the introduction of the concept of place value. Using two kinds of counters (ten of one equals one of the other), provide experiences for the child to trade them back and forth. The difficult part of the concept is to understand that 1 in any column is broken apart and becomes 10 when moved one column to the right. One in the tens column becomes 10 in the ones column. It is usually easier for a child to understand bundling up ten 1s to become one group of 10 than to envision a single 10 becoming ten 1s. Begin by laying out counters to represent two-digit numbers using two kinds of counters to represent 1s and 10s. Build the connections between the spoken word, the written number symbol, and the layout of manipulatives. Intersperse laying out the number in just 1s and converting it to 10s and 1s. Progress to having the child lay out two two-digit numbers that, when totaled, require converting 1s to 10s (for example, 16 plus 14 or 27 plus 34). Time spent with manipulatives at this stage of development pays off in terms of understanding when you move on to paper

and pencil calculations. By manipulating objects, the child can more easily visualize the relationships between 1s, 10s, and 100s.

- The next step is to demonstrate place value in subtraction. Give the child a verbal prompt such as 23 take away 4. Using counters to represent 10s and 1s, have the child lay out the two-digit number and remove counters representing the single-digit number. In the process the child will have to regroup, replacing a 10s counter with ten 1s. As skill develops, introduce subtracting a two-digit number from another two-digit number. When the child truly understands regrouping with two-digit numbers, expanding to three- and four-digit numbers follows logically.

ESTIMATING

The National Council of Teachers of Mathematics includes the skill of estimation among its priorities. Estimating is a practical skill that we use more often than we realize. In many cases, an exact calculation is not as necessary as an accurate estimate. On a daily basis, individuals make estimations related to time and distance, size and quantity, temperature, or running totals. Do I have enough time to vacuum before picking the kids up at school? Are there enough leftovers to make another meal? Is this box big enough to package a particular item? Is it cold enough to need a coat? Do I have enough money to include ice cream in my shopping cart? In each of these instances, you don't need the exact figure, but rather the ability to estimate. Learning to estimate is an acquired skill that improves with practice. When you use it, share and discuss with the child

how you do it. For example, recognizing that you are being overcharged for a purchase because what you are asked
to pay varies significantly from the total that was mentally
estimated. Errors in mathematical calculation are recognizable when the answer is unreasonable compared to the
estimate. The problem may be in the estimation or the calculation, but a discrepancy suggests the need to recheck.

Prerequisite Skills

- An emerging sense of measuring time, distance, quantity, size, temperature, weight.

Concepts

- There is a difference between exact calculation and
  approximation.
- Sometimes a calculated answer is appropriate, sometimes an estimation is.

Materials

- Nothing special; simply take advantage of opportunities in daily life as they present themselves.

Procedures

- Become creative when interacting with the child. Look
  for situations that will allow the child to make estimations and then verify them to see how accurate the
  estimate was. Sample situations and prompts include:

- How many Lego™ pieces will fit into a particular container?
- How many counters can you pick up in one handful?
- When taking silverware from the drawer to set the table, attempt to take the exact number without counting.
- How many spoonfuls will it take to finish your cereal?
- How long will it take you to clean your room?
- How long can you hold your breath?
- How many steps will it take to walk across the room?
- Which of two items do you think will weigh more (or less)?
- Arrange items according to weight (light to heavy, or vice-versa).

Extensions

- More advanced estimations involve rounding numbers up and down, and mentally calculating answers to mathematical problems.
- The estimated answer should be checked for reasonableness.

GRAPHING

Graphing provides a visual representation of information. A great deal of information is presented in graphic formats; therefore, it is essential to be able to interpret them. Graphs can take many forms ranging from the simplest pictograph to bar, line, or circle graphs. Graphing requires one to analyze and organize the data in order to present it. This requires comprehension of the data, relationships, and formats. Similar skills are needed to interpret graphs as to create them. Graphs can be constructed by hand or computer. However it is done, the child needs to comprehend the relationships between data and format (range, labels, amounts, etc.)

Prerequisite Skills

- Ability to count.
- Comprehension of greater than and less then.
- Understanding of sequential order.

Concepts

- Create a range that includes the extremes of the data.
- Determine units to be used in representation of data.
- Interpret grid coordinates.
- Recognize the need for titles and labels.

Materials

- Collection of data to graph.
- Materials to construct the graph.

Procedures

- The simplest graphing format is a pictograph. For a first exercise, graph the furniture in the house. Count the number of chairs, beds, tables, couches, chests. On 3x5 cards, draw a picture or symbol, paste pictures from catalogs, or rubber stamp a representation of each piece of furniture, with only one symbol on each card. Place the completed cards beside each other in categories. You can easily convert this pictograph into a bar graph by adding labels and a range of numbers. Other items to graph might be favorite foods, types of clothing, colors or shapes of items.

- A more sophisticated topic for graphing might be the part of a plant you are eating when you eat different vegetables. Columns in the graph might be root, stem, leaf, seed, seedpod (fruit), and flower. Limit the range to ten items. Color in each bar to represent the number of vegetables that fit each category.
- Survey playmates or relatives to collect data regarding favorite pets, TV shows, cars, foods, colors, and so on, and present the resulting data in a graph.

Extensions

- Use line and circle graphs for the same data.
- Introduce how to read a graph on which points do not coincide with identified points on the range. If the range is by fives and the point is between ten and fifteen, determine which it is closer to and how much closer in order to determine the specific value. (In pictographs, interpret the value of fractional picture units.)
- When reading published graphs, be alert to the key that provides the value for each symbol. In a pictograph, one symbol (a dog) might represent one or ten or even one-hundred dogs. So if multiple dogs are shown, the total value has to be multiplied.

FRACTIONS

Fractions are understood intuitively before direct instruction occurs. We divide candy bars; we slice pizzas, cakes, and pies; we pour a quart of milk into glasses. Things are shared by dividing the whole into parts. The more people, the more parts that are needed and the smaller the piece. Direct instruction provides vocabulary for naming these pieces: whole, halves, thirds, quarters, eighths, and so on. Stories such as *The Doorbell Rang* provide opportunities to discuss concepts related to fractions.

Prerequisite Skills

- The ability to count.
- The concept of equality.

Concepts

- Develop the meaning of numerator and denominator. The denominator is the total number of pieces the whole is divided into, and the numerator is the number of pieces you are working with.
- The greater the number in the denominator, the more pieces the whole has been broken into; therefore each piece is smaller.
- The fraction indicates size in relationship to the whole. A half of a postage stamp is smaller than a quarter of an envelope. Actual size is relative.
- The fraction parts of a whole must be of identical size.

Materials

- Things to cut up or divide into fractional parts.

Procedures

- Talk about dividing things such as cutting the sandwich into halves or quarters; the glass is half-full of milk.
- Use counters and divide them into fractional parts.
- Fold laundry in half, thirds, or quarters. Discuss fractions by counting the total number of shirts in the load and identifying a fractional part represented by a specific number of shirts.
- Discuss fractions while preparing recipes.
- Discuss fractions while playing in the bathtub by filling and emptying containers.

Extensions

- Convert fractions to the lowest common denominator: 2/10 is the same as 1/5, or 3/3 equals a whole.
- Examine the relationship between coins and their fractional part of a dollar.
- Examine the relationship between minutes and their fractional part of an hour.
- Identify fractional relationships between days, weeks, months, years, decades, centuries.

Chapter 7

Science

Young children have a natural curiosity about the world around them. Opportunities to develop the building blocks for the scientific process are all around the house and yard. Take the time with children to observe phenomena and explain what they see happening. Ask questions that lead them to make predictions, draw conclusions, and then verify them through observations and data collection. These steps will help establish the behaviors they need for more formal investigations of scientific concepts.

OBSERVATION

Seeing and observing are two very different activities. The dictionary defines to see as to perceive with the eyes. In contrast, to observe is defined as to see and notice, or to regard with attention while applying a methodical approach. The child needs to learn these differences and when to apply each process. The focus on providing hands-on science experiences for young children mandates that they learn to be observant while participating in them. One's ability to observe accurately and completely improves with practice. Give children constant opportunities for practice within normal activities. The key is being alert to and willing to spend the time necessary to take advantage of all that captures the child's interest.

Prerequisite Skills

- The vocabulary to verbalize what is observed.
- Sufficient attention span to stay focused after an initial look.

Concepts

- There is a difference between seeing and observing.
- The more one looks, the more one sees.
- There is specific vocabulary to match the phenomenon observed which needs to be learned.
- Using specific vocabulary for scientific concepts allows one to share observations with others.

Materials

- The world around you.
- Variety of containers suitable for holding items being observed.
- Books containing age-appropriate hands-on science activities as a source of ideas.

Procedures

- Talk with the child about the item that has captured the child's interest. Ask questions that elicit the need to make closer observations.
- Create situations that attract the child's attention to the observation of a scientific concept or principle. Encourage the child to try and explain it, and ask questions about what seems puzzling. Support further observation to try to generate and answer questions.
- Set up situations that require repeated observations over a period of time. Encourage the child to collect data throughout the experience.
- Use videotape footage to make observations of things and events not available for hands-on interaction. One advantage of using this format is that repeated viewing focuses the child's attention on what might have been missed initially, as well as on in-depth observations.

Extensions

- Take closeup snapshots of distinctive portions of familiar items. Ask the child to identify what the item is and where the actual item is located. Examples might include a doorknob, a recognizable crack in the sidewalk, the license plate of a vehicle, buttons on a coat, a page out of a book, a segment of fabric, floor coverings. Use a single example for a weekly scavenger hunt, or base an activity on a group of pictures.
- Make a list of jobs in which observation is an important element—for example, detectives, play-by-play

announcers for ball games, doctors, artists, farmers, actors.

- Provide living things that may be observed—plants, small animals or fish.
- Find unusual or historical objects, and ask the child to make observations to determine its probable use.

PREDICT AND VERIFY

Scientific discovery is based on prediction and verification. Accidental discoveries need to be replicated and verified. In either instance, it is vital to know how to construct a hypothesis and devise a process of proving if it is correct or incorrect. The inability to recognize what you do not know and to formulate it into a question holds one back in all areas, especially scientific inquiry. Once you recognize what you are trying to find out, you can design a procedure to acquire the needed information. The scientific process has applications across all disciplines, for we all are continually faced with verifying the status of situations and making decisions about how to proceed.

Prerequisite Skills

- Recognize cause-and-effect relationships.
- Recognize similarities and differences.
- Recognize sequential relationships.
- Comprehend known and unknown.

Concepts

- A prediction is an unproven assumption or best guess.
- Predictions need to be verified.
- "Hypothesis" is a scientific term for a prediction.

Materials

- Stories that invite the reader to make predictions and then read on to verify.
- A variety of materials with which to conduct scientific investigations in response to questions raised by the child.
- A collection of science activity books from which to pull ideas.

Procedures

- When reading stories, stop periodically and ask the child to predict the various possibilities of what might happen next. Continue reading to verify what really happens.
- In response to a question such as, "Which takes up more space, snow or water?" or "Will a plant grow in the dark?" ask the child to think of ways to find out the answer. Help them carry out the procedures they suggest and determine if the information acquired fully answers the question. Redesign the investigation if the initial approach did not fully answer the question, or raised additional questions to investigate.
- Demonstrate a scientific concept or principle that is designed to raise questions—such as how the egg got into the bottle, why the carnation changed colors,

what happened to the sugar dissolved in the water. Challenge the child to design an investigation that supports an hypothesis.

Extensions

- Investigate scientists and their inventions. Focus on the process they used to verify their hypotheses.
- Use materials like *The Way Things Work* or *How Things Work* to explore the scientific principles involved.
- Hold an "Invention Convention," in which each child creates an invention to solve a problem.
- Participate in local and regional competitions that can lead to national recognition, such as those sponsored by Invent America.

LIVING AND NONLIVING THINGS

A major method of categorizing things is whether they are living or nonliving entities. Living organisms are composed of cells and can grow and reproduce given a habitat that provides food, water, shelter, light, and rest. The study of living things is known as biology and is made up of botany (the study of plants) and zoology (the study of animals). Nonliving, or inanimate, objects include such natural things as rocks and minerals, and manufactured items such as metals, glass, or plastic, as well as constructions. Nonliving objects are unable to move or change on their own. Some of the sciences that study nonliving objects include geology, physics, astronomy, and inorganic chemistry.

Prerequisite Skills

- Use differences to categorize objects.

Concepts

- Not all things are living.
- There are requirements for sustaining life.
- Living things die, nonliving things do not.
- Being able to move, grow, change, and reproduce are attributes of life.
- Life exists in many different forms, and all deserve our respect.
- Protection of the environment is essential to life.

Materials

- The world around us.
- Pictures, books, videos, television programs focusing on the natural environment.

Procedures

- Identify those objects you interact with in daily life as living or nonliving. Discuss what you see on walks in the neighborhood or park.
- Plant seeds and observe the growth of a plant.
- Care for pets and observe their growth and development.
- Share books, videos, and television programs that focus on nature.

- Collect and categorize pictures of living and nonliving things.
- Collect actual objects such as rock specimens, shells, pressed leaves, or dry flowers.
- Participate in recycling and programs that help the environment.
- Visit a zoo, an aquarium, a farm, or other habitat in your area.

Extensions

- Explore differing habitats such as creeks, fields, wetlands, woods, shores, deserts.
- Identify and categorize living things by habitats such as rain forest, grassland, tundra, desert.
- Explore humane society activities and the problems of unwanted pets.
- Join an "adoption" program that saves endangered animals.

CHANGE AS A PROCESS

Change is an ever-occurring process by which things become different. Scientists observe change in order to explain phenomena and make predictions. Some change is cyclical, such as day into night or the seasons, the water cycle, tides, phases of the moon. Other change is linear, such as birth to death, the formation of fossil fuels from plant life, or the process of decay. Additional examples of change occurring in daily life include cooking of foods, puddles evaporating, ice melting to become water or steam, mixing colors to create a tint, knitting or sewing, or the growth of a plant or animal. Paint dries out and flakes off the wood, sawdust forms when wood is sawed, soil consistency changes with plowing. The philosopher Heraclitus has observed that the only constant thing in this world is change itself.

Prerequisite Skills

- The ability to notice that things are different.

Concepts

- Change is prevalent.
- Change may be cyclical or linear.
- Change can be replicated.
- Change can be influenced by adjusting the variables.
- Change can be observed.

Materials

- Tools for observing change, such as your own senses, magnifying glass, various kinds of containers, note-taking material, photographic material.
- Tools for creating change, such as those for cooking, cutting, growing, polishing, creating, constructing.

Procedures

- Take the time to help the child investigate the world around you, asking questions to focus attention on examples of change.

- Involve the child in observing foods before and after they are cooked and the changes that occur in texture, color, and taste as a result of peeling, slicing, stirring, mixing, baking, frying.
- Notice and talk about changes related to day and night, seasons, weather, things wearing out, and decay.
- Take photos of before and after situations to compare and contrast.
- Look for examples of change in stories that you share.
- Engage the child in simple science experiments that produce change such as growing crystals or molds, friction (rolling toy cars across carpeted and hard surfaces), dissolving substances such as salt or sugar, testing for floating and sinking. Consult science fair–type books for ideas.
- Share science-related television programs or web sites and highlight any elements of change they cover.

Extensions

- Document examples of change around you. Keep a log of your own height and weight, daily weather record, or other situations you like to keep track of, such as the growth of a sibling or pet.
- Look into how transportation, communication, architecture, dress, art, or music has changed throughout time.
- Make a list of sports records and how often they are broken.
- Make a list of ways in which your own interests and abilities have changed over time.

- Identify changes you would like to make, things you look forward to being able to do.

CAUSE AND EFFECT

The relationship between cause and effect can be observed or inferred. The child can find evidence of cause-and-effect relationships in daily life in situations as obvious as carelessness causing an accident or the consequences of appropriate or inappropriate behaviors. Once one understands cause and effect, one recognizes that one's own actions impact on others, which is a first step toward accepting responsibility. Once the concept of cause and effect is learned, you can identify scientific applications: putting water into the freezer produces ice cubes; heavy rain runoff creates erosion in the yard; gravity causes round things to roll downhill. The recognition of such relationships helps to provide a structure for organizing information.

Prerequisite Skills

- The ability to see that there are connections between things rather than that events are purely random.

Concepts

- "Cause" produces a result.
- "Effect" is the result of something having happened.
- There is a relationship between specific causes and their effects.

Materials

- Experiences in daily life.
- Books that contain simple science experiments.
- Household items to support experiments.

Procedures

- Verbalize examples of cause and effect as they occur in daily life.
- Discuss with the child examples of cause and effect in which the child is directly involved, such as how eating relieves hunger, washing hands removes dirt, following directions reduces reprimands.
- Encourage the child to recognize and explain any examples of cause and effect observed.
- Create situations in which the cause-and-effect relationship is evident, and discuss them with the child.
- Move on to creating simple scientific experiments.

Extensions

- Explore less concrete examples from such sources as the evening news, weather forecasting, or plots of stories.
- Predict the consequences or results of real or hypothetical situations—for example, if you leave your toys in the driveway, if you ignore safety practices (touch a hot stove, cross the street without looking, put your hand or foot into moving machinery), or if you wander away from your adult in a public place.

DRAWING CONCLUSIONS

The conclusion is the last step in a chain of reasoning formed after investigation and thought. This is the culmination of becoming able to organize data gathered in a variety of ways. It is the summarizing of what has gone before and is based on logic and facts. The problem arises in assuring accuracy of the conclusion reached. Facts can be misinterpreted; for example, a group of kindergarten students came to the conclusion that when tadpoles get their legs they die. The problem was that these tadpoles were toads, not frogs, and because they had nothing to climb out on they drowned. Their conclusion fit their observations, but they were basing their conclusion on insufficient information. All tadpoles do not become frogs. Children need to draw their own conclusions, but they also need to be led to correct any misconceptions.

Prerequisite Skills

- Experience with making observations, prediction, verification, identifying cause and effect, and sources of change.

Concepts

- Record data you have collected to study for interpretation later.
- Inference is based on known facts or evidence, but it requires the added element of making valid assumptions.

- An accurate conclusion must account for all the data collected.
- Conclusions need to be tested and verified and not accepted without evaluation.

Materials

- Materials for recording collected data ranging from notebook to tape recorder or laptop computer.
- Basic tools for measuring, collecting, and observing.
- Library books for sources of ideas.
- The world around you for drawing conclusions related to observations.

Procedures

- Provide opportunities for the child to make observations, record data, and draw and test conclusions—for example, data related to planting and sprouting seeds, melting ice cubes (on a dish, in glass of cold or hot water), the relationship between the size of a base and the height of a tower built with blocks, daily weather, things that float or sink.
- Ask questions that lead the child to draw conclusions related to stories shared, occurrences in daily life, televised events.

Extensions

- Encourage the child to devise ways of testing conclusions. For example, rubber is waterproof, so the child might test boot waterproofness by walking in puddles or wading in the bathtub. To test that snow takes up more space than water, fill a container with snow and let it melt. The point is that the child devises the method of testing the conclusion.

- Introduce the child to the science of logic through the use of syllogisms, a form of reasoning in which two statements are made and a logical conclusion is drawn from them. For example, mammals are warm blooded, whales are mammals; therefore, whales are warm blooded.

- Using examples of correct and incorrect reasoning, let the child recognize errors in reasoning.

Chapter 8

Geography

Geography becomes increasingly important as individuals come to appreciate their place in a global society. As barriers of time and distance are removed through the growth of technology, the development of geographic literacy enables individuals to comprehend their interdependence with the rest of the world as well as the global impact of their own actions. Geography is no longer limited to the memorization of lists of places and the ability to locate them on a map. A geographically informed person understands the nature of physical systems—ecology—and the influence they have on earth as a setting for human life.

The evolving definition of geography encompasses a broad range of concepts—for example, the spatial aspects of the world involve not only where physical and political entities are located, but also how they are arranged, why they are in such locations, and how they relate to each other. In addition, geography also involves the study of physical systems that shape and reshape land forms (weather, erosion, earthquakes, and volcanoes) in conjunction with human systems that occur as people move, settle, develop economic interchanges, and initiate systems of cooperation and conflict.

Environmental modifications by human action will continue to be a dominant concern in the next century. The ramifications will be recognized only by geographically literate individuals who understand the interactions among physical systems, human systems, and the environment (Salter 1995).

NEIGHBORHOOD

As children's horizons broaden, they become aware of areas beyond their own home and yard. The nearest ones are those of the neighborhood. As the child accompanies adults on errands, they begin to recognize the sites that are routinely visited for basic goods and services such as grocery store, gas station, bank, post office, mall, school, park, and so on. The child also begins to recognize specific people and identifies them as neighbors. As experience increases, a child may start to observe distinguishing characteristics shared by residents of the neighborhood as well as of the neighborhood itself. The significant adults in the child's life need to help the child overcome any negative element and to take advantage of the positive elements that help the child develop a sense of belonging, neighborliness, and community.

Prerequisite Skills

- Able to recognize similarities and differences.
- Has begun to associate current and past repetitive experiences.

Concepts

- Associate activities with establishments—e.g., buying food at the grocery, mailing packages at the post office; borrowing books from the library.
- There is a pattern to streets and paths that connects home with other locations.
- Although there may be a number of ways to get from one place to another, there are advantages and disadvantages to each such as time, distance, safety, or special interests.

Materials

- The world around you; go to local establishments and take the time to include the child on the errands.

Procedures

- Talk to the child about what you need, why you chose the establishment, and how you are getting there.
- If walking, verbalize the decisions you are making as you arrive at intersections or other points of choice; if using public transportation or driving, identify clues you are using to find your way, such as signage or distinctive landmarks.
- As awareness increases, have the child identify the establishment that fits a need and give directions for getting there, describing the clues used.

Extensions

- Take photographs of neighborhood locations and use these for discussions, such as what you see in the photo; for sequencing, such as distance from home, favorite to least favorite place to go, alphabetical order, or for matching location with function.
- Place your local neighborhood in the context of a larger community. Introduce the concepts of residential, commercial, recreational elements within a community.
- Introduce the concepts of rural, suburban, and urban areas.

MAIL

Mail provides an inexpensive method of communicating across great distances. With this service, provided by the government and also by commercial companies, one can send packages as well as letters. To send an item, however, you need to know a person's complete address. Then you need to purchase stamps and attach them to the item to prove that fees have been paid according to weight and speed of delivery. Because of the diverse geographic locations represented by postmarks and stamps, collecting can be an interesting hobby.

Prerequisite Skills

- Understanding of the elements related to the process of mail service.
- The concept that mail is delivered according to a schedule.

Concepts

- On an envelope, identify stamp, postmark, address, and return address.
- The United States Postal Service or other commercial delivery services transport letters or packages so you don't have to take them yourself.
- International deliveries depend upon cooperation between countries that provide similar services.
- Stamps are purchased in the country from which the mail is sent. They can be used only in the country issuing them.
- There are standard abbreviations that must be understood in order to effectively address an item.
- Abbreviations for place names used on stamps and postmarks represent actual locations on a map or globe.
- Mail addressed to a person should only be opened by that person; it is personal property.

Materials

- Examples of stamps, postmarks, addresses from mail received and mail being sent.
- United States and world maps; a globe.

Procedures

- Analyze stamps, postmarks, and addresses to identify an item's country or state of origin.
- Locate these on appropriate maps and globes.
- Discuss the relationship between the time it took to deliver the item and the distance traveled.

- Categorize mail according to first class, personal, advertising, junk, catalogs, magazines. Point out what types of mail are addressed to just occupant or resident as opposed to items bearing an individual's name.
- Emphasize to the child that mail should be handled with respect and not treated as a toy. It is for the person to whom it is addressed and no one else.

Extensions

- Take advantage of the increase in personal greetings at holiday times. Cut out postmarks and plot them on a map.
- Involve the child when you are using specialized services such as insured, registered, certified, overnight express, or customs declarations for international delivery.
- Help the child start a stamp collection.

FOODS

The variety of foods available in today's grocery stores reflects the global nature of society. Ethnic specialties appear everywhere; fresh fruits and vegetables, canned and packaged items, baked goods, spices are imported from all parts of the world to supply the demands of the buying public. Not only is there demand from ethnic groups for their own tastes, but there is also a growing interest among people to learn to prepare and enjoy a wide variety of foods. In a similar fashion, interest in ethnic restaurants has also increased.

Prerequisite Skills

- A willingness to "experiment"—to try a wide variety of unfamiliar foods.

Concepts

- Foods come from plants and animals.
- Different foods are produced in different parts of the world.
- Basic nutritional needs must be met for good health regardless of the specific dietary item or its preparation.

Materials

- Foods purchased for family meals.
- Cookbooks for recipes.
- Meals eaten at ethnic restaurants to sample their specialties.
- Reference materials to locate place of origin for menu items.
- Library books to share that include references to foods. For example, *Cloudy with a Chance of Meatballs, The Giant Jam Sandwich, How to Make an Apple Pie and See the World,* and *How My Parents Learned to Eat.*

Procedures

- When shopping in the grocery store, examine and talk about unusual foods and where they come from.

- Buy and prepare examples of previously unfamiliar foods.
- Continue talking at the table about the geographic aspects of meals you've prepared and that are being eaten by the family.
- Use a system of small "no thank-you helpings" to encourage the child to taste unfamiliar foods.
- When sharing library books look for opportunities to talk about food items and their role in the story. Don't overlook illustrations.

Extensions

- Eat out at ethnic restaurants from time to time.
- View televised cooking shows that focus on the preparation of ethnic foods.
- Start making connections between the part of the plant you are eating when you eat various fruits and vegetables—e.g., root, stem, leaf, flower, seed, seed pod.
- Identify the kind of animal, or part of an animal, that provides various cuts of meat.
- Identify similarities in construction of food items around the world such as variations on sandwiches or egg rolls and burritos.

HOLIDAYS

There are similarities among holidays celebrated by various cultures. For example, most cultures honor birthdays, weddings, anniversaries of historical events, the harvest, the new year, and spring's arrival in addition to their preferred religious celebrations. The specifics of the celebrations may vary, but their underlying themes are universal. Special foods, costumes, activities, decorations, music, dances, and stories are all associated with the celebration of holidays. Often these elements identify the culture or ethnic group participating in the celebration.

Prerequisite Skills

- Experience with your own group's celebrations in order to make comparisons with those of other groups.

Concepts

- There are many ways to celebrate universal themes.
- Climate as well as ethnic backgrounds influence local celebrations.
- Holidays happen throughout the year.
- Some holidays are shared by people around the world, and others are regional or individual family affairs.

Materials

- Storybooks, cookbooks, videos, recordings, audio- and videotapes that provide background for ethnic celebrations.

Procedures

- Explain what your family does as part of popular celebrations and share their background and history.

- Establish new traditions that become a part of your family's observances.
- Look at other cultures' traditions that are practiced by people in the neighborhood or community.
- Share stories, songs, dances, foods, costumes that reflect practices from around the world.

Extensions

- Discuss family traditions and celebrations related to various holidays that are *unique to your family*. Explain how they got started and why you keep them.
- Participate in public events that reflect a variety of ethnic celebrations.
- Use maps and globes to locate countries whose celebrations are included in television news coverage of holidays, such as Chinese New Year or Japanese Children's Day; or more local sites, such as Punxsutawney Phil's home in connection with Groundhog Day, or Hinckley, Ohio, for the annual return of the buzzards.

TRANSPORTATION

Transportation is the means of moving goods and people from one place to another. The design of the vehicle is determined by its purpose and whether it is for use on land, air, or water. Some vehicles are for mass transportation, and others are for individual use.

There has been an historical progression in transportation from dependence on muscle power to the use of mechanical devices. As the global nature of society has evolved, the need for faster, cheaper, safer means of moving people and goods has become a priority. The ability to ship perishable goods means that we can now buy year-round items that once were only available seasonally. Transportation has facilitated leisure travel and tourism.

Prerequisite Skills

- Recognition that different modes of transportation exist.

Concepts

- The mode of transportation matches the requirements of a trip, including time, distance, weight, bulk, perishability, and cost.
- Goods as well as people need to be transported.
- Vehicles are continually being invented, modified, improved to meet the demands of transportation needs.

Materials

- Concrete experiences with a variety of modes of transportation.
- Pictures and model versions of vehicles.

Procedures

- Discuss the transportation being used by the characters in stories you read together.

- When traveling, discuss the decisions made and why you are using the vehicles you are using.
- Role play with toy cars, trucks, planes, ships, and so on.
- Brainstorm how transportation helped get the items you wish to purchase onto the shelves of a store.
- If purchasing large items, figure out what is involved in getting them home.
- When ordering from a catalog, explain the reasons for shipping and handling charges.
- While watching television or movies, talk about transportation concepts incorporated in the story.
- Collect pictures from magazines and catalogs related to transportation methods. Categorize and sequence these pictures in various ways.
- Match the mode of transportation with the needs of moving a specific product, such as cars from Japan to the United States, diamonds from South Africa to New York, fruits and vegetables from South America to your grocery store. Discuss time, distance, weight, perishability, and cost.

Extensions

- Visit museums featuring displays related to transportation, such as the Smithsonian's Air and Space Museum, which permits one to walk through space vehicles.
- Design vehicles using construction toys and readily available materials such as boxes, spools, buttons, paper towel tubes, and the like. Discuss the characteristics of the vehicle designed.

STREET ADDRESSES

Once the child can recognize "home," it becomes important to emphasize that specific locations can be identified. The child needs as soon as possible to be able to verbalize the family name, street address, and phone number so that, in the event of an unexpected separation from adults while away from home, the child can communicate these facts. Give the child plenty of practice in this so that the response becomes automatic.

Prerequisite Skills

- Recognize difference between letters and numbers.
- Recognize the format of a phone number and of an address.
- Recognize differences between family and given names.

Concepts

- Your last name identifies you as a member of a family group.
- Your first name identifies you as an individual within that group.
- A phone number has a three-digit area code, followed by a three-digit exchange, followed by four digits in a specific order. Any variation in sequence connects with a different location.
- A street address consists of number, name, and type of roadway—street, court, boulevard, avenue, terrace, road, drive, parkway, circle, and the like.

- A complete address frequently requires the use of a location code, such as a zip code in the United States or international postal equivalents.

Materials

- Items that show the use of address and phone number information in daily life:
  — the numbers on the mailbox, house, and street signs
  — envelopes from delivered mail
  — the phone book
  — a personal address book
  — a luggage tag.

Procedures

- Point out instances when you use your address and phone number.
- Talk about how such information assists in mail and other delivery services.
- Help the child learn to say his/her full name and parents' names; next, learn to repeat the phone number; continue by learning to repeat the street address.
- Using a game type format that is fun encourages the child to master these important facts. Once the child can repeat the information, continue to practice to maintain the automatic nature of the response.

Extensions

- Recognize the information in printed form and learn to read and write it.
- Add town, state, and zip code to provide a complete mailing address.
- Explore the concept of e-mail and web-site addresses.

CONTINENT, COUNTRY, STATE, CITY

The terms and related ideas associated with the standard political divisions constitute basic geographic knowledge. These concepts are difficult for young children to grasp when they have not had the actual experience of travel. However, it is important to be able to recognize the relationships among these categories and become able to relate terms heard in current events with appropriate concepts regarding political divisions. The mere memorization of lists of place names is meaningless. A place name needs to be augmented with a meaningful context of location, culture, climate, and human interest elements to make sense of the name, to make it useful.

Prerequisite Skills

- Knowledge that there are labels for certain kinds of things.
- The function of labels is to identify categories.
- Realization that similarities exist among the elements that fit within a category.
- Realization that there are names for places in the world.

Concepts

- Develop the concepts of city, state, country, and continent.
- Differentiate among the concepts city, state, country, continent.
- Match specific examples to the appropriate concepts.

Materials

- Globes and/or world maps.
- Country maps, state maps.
- Stories set in other countries.
- Pictures and postcards of recognizable city symbols and monuments.

Procedures

- Start with a globe. Identify the name and location of each of the seven continents.
- Point out how color represents countries within continents.
- Give the names of some countries. If families or friends live abroad, link them to that country or continent.
- Focus on the United States. Examine maps to show how the country is made up of smaller segments, and that these are states.
- Locate your own state and states where relatives or friends live.
- Introduce the idea of cities. Locate major cities around the world. Discuss the relationships between cities, countries, states, and continents.

- When reading stories and folk tales, look for clues that identify the settings and locate them on the globe.
- Do the same thing when watching films or television. If starting with a city, work your way back to state, country, continent.

CARDINAL DIRECTIONS

Interpretation of the four chief directions of the compass is a basic skill. The compass was known by the Chinese and the Mediterraneans as early as the year 1000 and used in navigation. Now markedly improved, the compass remains the basic navigational tool. Even though most of us are not navigators, we do incorporate the relationships among north, south, east, and west in a variety of daily life activities. We place plants in particular spots in the garden or on the windowsill depending upon the sun's orientation. We frequently consult a map when driving. Orienteering as a sport, hiking, and camping all offer chances to use a simple compass.

Prerequisite Skills

- Understand the relationships between up and down, right and left.
- Comprehend the meaning of opposite.

Concepts

- North, south, east, and west are the names of directions.

- North and south are opposite directions, and so are east and west.
- The linking of north with up, south with down, east with right, and west with left.

Materials

- Maps, pictures.
- Concrete experiences with the location of the sun and your location.

Procedures

- Observe where the sun rises and sets.
- Raise the child's awareness that the sun is not always shining into the same window throughout the day.
- Track how one's shadow changes throughout the day. Correlate the position of shadows with cardinal directions and location of the sun.
- With a compass, figure out which side of the house faces which direction.
- Share examples of simple maps.
- Explain the need to orient a map appropriately in order to have accurate information.
- Introduce the convention of north being the top of the map, and so forth.
- Use pictures to identify directional relationships among objects. Ask questions such as, "What object is north of the cat, car, boat?" "What direction would the cat walk to get to the tree?" or "What animal is south and east of the barn?"

Extensions

- Introduce the intercardinal directions of northeast, northwest, southeast, southwest, and points in-between.
- Prompt the child to guess what time of day it is based on the location of the sun in a picture (sunset, sunrise, morning, afternoon).
- Figure out the directional orientation of a picture based on the location of the sun and time of day.
- Use your place setting at the dinner table to practice recognizing directional relationships. Using the convention of north being top, the glass is northeast of the plate, or the spoon is east of the plate and the fork is west of it.
- Create simple maps that show familiar places in the community. Label the map with north, south, east, west.

MAPPING

Map reading is a basic skill. Finding an unfamiliar location frequently involves interpreting formal or informal maps. Following the basic directional orientation, one needs to be able to interpret standard symbols and scale. In time, basic map-reading skills transfer to reading more specialized maps with unique purposes such as topographical, product, or star maps, and navigational or ocean current charts.

Prerequisite Skills

- Knowledge of cardinal directions.
- Recognition that a map represents actual locations.
- Understanding the use of symbols to represent concrete objects.
- Realizing the role of scale in representing large objects.

Concepts

- Locations on a map match the real thing (e.g., a railroad crossing, a bridge over a river, or a school).
- There are relationships between locations on a map that represent distance, direction, and the time required to get from one place to another.
- Standard map symbols mean certain things, such as expressways versus backroads, capitol cities versus towns, parks, bodies of water, schools, libraries, hospitals, airports, and the like.
- The ability to use scale symbols to determine actual distances.

Materials

- An assortment of maps, including road maps, handdrawn neighborhood sketches, endpages, and literary maps found in storybooks.
- Atlases (to expand concept of maps).
- Globes.

Procedures

- Any time you are using a map, make a point of talking about map use.
- Create maps that reflect the route you use to go to familiar places.
- Follow along a map as you travel.
- Point out maps that appear on coupons and in magazines and newspapers.
- If an acquaintance is making a business or pleasure trip, plot the route on a map.
- If you receive postcards, locate where they were mailed and how long they took to arrive.
- When planning your own vacation trip, incorporate maps. Identify symbols that indicate roadside rest stops, parks, route changes, railroads, bridges and river crossings, historic sites, points of interest, or whatever is appropriate along your route.

Extensions

- Explore specialized maps and the information they provide.
- Create maps to reflect experiences, real or fictional. Examples can be found in *The Dictionary of Imaginary Places*.
- Explore the use of coordinate grids to locate a position on a map.

COORDINATES

Coordinates identify the location of a point on a line, on a surface, or in space. A system of coordinates using letters and numbers is commonly used on maps to assist in finding a specific location listed in the map index. The system superimposes a grid over the map labeling the horizontal and vertical lines with letters and numbers. The index gives a location code for a site, for example B4 or G10, and you follow the two lines to their intersection to locate it. The item being sought will be close to this point on the map. When it's the space between the lines that is labeled, the intersection creates a box in which to look rather than a point. By skimming words within the box, the item can be found.

Prerequisite Skills

- A concept of up and down as well as side to side.
- A concept of intersection.
- Able to determine alphabetical order.
- Knowing numerical order.

Concepts

- Vertical is the term used for up and down.
- Horizontal is the term used for side to side.
- Horizontal and vertical lines intersect.
- A point can be identified through the use of coordinates.

Materials

- Yarn, ribbon, string, or markers and chart paper to create grids.
- Collection of pictures from catalogs, advertisements, greeting cards, and the like.
- Labels for the grid.
- Maps to use to apply grid concepts.

Procedures

- Create a simple grid of no more than five rows and columns by drawing lines on a piece of paper or taping strips of yarn, ribbon, or string, to a floor or table. Label the rows and columns using letters for one and numbers for the other. Place a distinctive picture in each box on the grid.
- Ask the child to point to a specific picture. Explain the grid coordinate letter and number labels that identify the box that contains that picture. Once the child appears to grasp the process, provide a grid coordinate code and ask the child to locate the picture that it identifies. Continue to practice alternating the format of prompts.
- Increase the complexity of the grid to include additional rows and columns. Incorporate more sophisticated pictures, or use words instead of pictures as the child begins to read.
- Transfer the process to finding locations on actual maps.

Extensions

- Longitude and latitude are terms for a specialized grid on maps. They create coordinates and they intersect. Degrees, minutes, and seconds make these measurements highly accurate. These measurements are used in navigation on land, sea, and air.

Chapter 9

Economics

An "economically literate" person realizes that most people want to own more than they can afford to purchase, and most that nations are no different. The interdependence of producers and consumers is the basis of economics. The cycle of earning and spending money determines the ways goods and services are produced, distributed, and consumed. People and nations learn to economize in order to have the most possible of what they need and/or want. Deciding on how to economize is a very important skill that has impact on supply and demand—elements that affect wages and what is produced, as well as the prices paid for those items.

MONEY

Money is an agreed-upon medium of exchange, usually paper bills or metal coins, that people accept as payment for things they sell or work they do. Each country has its own currency with distinctive markings, shapes, and values. Money allows individuals to store wealth for use at a future time. To be convenient, money should come in pieces of standard value so that they do not have to be weighed or measured each time they are used. Money should be easy to carry and divide into units so that change can be made as needed. Currencies from different countries can be exchanged for each other based on an exchange rate influenced by world conditions.

Prerequisite Skills

- Recognition of money as something of value.
- Able to distinguish subtle differences between similar objects.
- Aware of differences between real money and play money.

Concepts

- Recognize the vocabulary of money, naming specific coins and bills.
- Match specific coins and bills with their names and values.
- Understand the relationships among different coins and bills.

Materials

- Real money.
- Play money.
- Items that can create play store or bank situations.

Procedures

- Start by using your country's real money so the children can learn to identify coins and match them to their values.
- Match values of coins to assorted prices.
- Practice making change up to one dollar.
- Repeat these activities using bills of small denominations.
- Incorporate role play buying and selling into these activities.
- Involve the child with actual purchases by supervising their handling of money and waiting for accurate change.

Extensions

- Give the child experience with independently handling money through use of allowances and savings accounts.
- Introduce the idea of using checks in place of actual money.
- Introduce the advantages and disadvantages of credit cards and debit cards.
- Share samples of foreign currency you may have acquired through travel.

COMMUNITY HELPERS

Community helpers provide the goods and services that both individual people and the community at large need. The training required and status received may vary, but all community helpers contribute to the general welfare. Some workers are employed by the government, and others are employed by commercial concerns or are self-employed entrepreneurs.

Prerequisite Skills

- Recognize that jobs fulfill the needs of the community.
- Recognize the relationship between working and getting paid for work.

Concepts

- To keep the community functioning requires a wide range of jobs.
- Some services are provided to everyone by the government, for example, policemen, firemen, teachers, judges, librarians.
- Commercially sponsored services require payment when used, for example work done by the hairdresser, the car mechanic, the doctor, or the dentist.

Materials

- Books from the library about community helpers.
- The community at large.

Procedures

- Identify various community helpers as you interact with them.

- Talk with the child about workers' responsibilities and appropriate interactions with them.
- Categorize community helpers in a variety of ways— for example, medical, safety, recreation, food services, education, maintenance, landscaping, sanitation.
- Read books about careers.

Extensions

- Talk about the child's future career choices and requirements.
- Discuss similarities and differences between the concepts of careers and community helpers—not all careers are directly related to the welfare of the community.

WANTS AND NEEDS

Individuals need to recognize the differences between what one truly needs to survive and what one wants to enhance life style. Most people's incomes require them to make choices as to what they purchase. It is important to place priority on fulfilling needs before wants. The message of advertising often is that one can immediately have what one wants without identifying long-term costs. Little is said about the advantage of saving in advance for making a purchase rather than engaging in the increased costs that come with using credit. Such behaviors can be introduced when the child is deciding how to spend an allowance. Discussing the results and impact of choices made helps build an awareness of the relationship between spending patterns and economic reality.

Prerequisite Skills

- Understanding the relationship between earning money and the ability to make purchases.
- Recognizing that one may not get everything one wants.

Concepts

- Distinguish between wants and needs.

Materials

- Collection of pictures from advertisements or catalogs.

Procedures

- Categorize the pictures according to needs and wants.
- Sequence the pictures according to priority of wants.
- Review the family budget and its implications prior to shopping trips.
- Discuss name brands versus house brands in terms of value versus cost.
- Talk about and explain merchandising tactics designed to increase purchases.
- If possible, provide the child with an allowance and develop guidelines for its use. Make it clear to the child if there is anything that must be purchased from the allowance or if it is totally a discretionary fund. Discuss ways of saving for a larger more lasting purchase as opposed to buying consumables.

Extensions

- Establish a savings account in the child's name at the local bank.
- Discuss spending patterns you see in television or films.
- Develop "wish lists" using advertisements or prices from stores, and calculate the items' actual costs.
- Compare the real cost of using credit to an outright purchase.
- Analyze the real cost of mail order purchases when shipping and handling are included. Include the added cost of returning unsatisfactory items.

GOODS AND SERVICES

When making purchases, one receives either goods or services: goods are tangible objects, services are things people do for you. The price one pays for goods or services is determined by how much it costs the provider to produce or provide it plus a profit margin.

Prerequisite Skills

- Recognition that special skills are required to do certain jobs.
- Ability to identify things you cannot do or make for yourself and thus must pay others to do or make for you.

Concepts

- Goods are tangible objects.
- Services are jobs others do for you either because you cannot do them yourself or because you are willing to pay for the convenience of having the job done for you.
- Goods and services can be bought and sold.

Materials

- The community at large.
- Ads for goods and services from newspapers and mailings.

Procedures

- When making purchases in various businesses discuss the variety of goods and services provided. Identify your purchases as being goods or services. For example, at the gas station, goods would include gas, oil, tires, and services would include repairs, oil changes, filling the tank, washing the windshield (i.e., the difference between self-service and full-service). At the post office, you buy a roll of stamps (goods) that purchases a service (delivery of letters at a later date).

Extensions

- Discuss the concept of "free." Is there such a thing?
- Investigate the training or schooling required to prepare one to provide services as a career; for example, auto mechanic, banker, hair stylist, doctor, plumber.

PRODUCERS AND CONSUMERS

Production is the first step in a series of economic processes that bring goods and services to consumers. Producers are the people who grow or manufacture products. Consumers are people who use goods and services. Examples of consumption include eating food, wearing clothes, and using soap. The amount of goods and services consumed by a family is largely dependent upon its size and income. The process of producing a product such as a box of cereal demonstrates how one's role can alternate between that of being a producer and a consumer. The farmer is a producer of corn, but a consumer of fertilizer. The factory produces corn flakes but is a consumer of machinery, corn, and paper boxes. The truck driver who distributes the cornflakes is a consumer of gas and tires and at the same time is a producer delivering the cereal to the storekeeper. On the job, one is a producer earning wages, but one becomes a consumer when purchasing items with these wages. It is the interaction between producers and consumers that keeps the economy healthy.

Prerequisite Skills

- Comprehension that things are "made" and do not just "happen."
- Understanding that things are consumable and need to be replaced, for example, milk or detergent; clothing, which wears out or is outgrown.

Concepts

- There are differences between making and using products.
- Independence and interdependence are different.
- There is an historical progression from self-sufficiency to interdependence.
- The quality of products improves with specialization.
- Mass production reduces costs.

Materials

- The products that surround one.

Procedures

- Analyze what is involved in producing various everyday products. Discuss the sources of natural resources and the processing and distribution required to provide the product for the consumer.
- Compare and contrast products you might make for yourself with those available for purchase. It is possible to spin your own wool and weave your own cloth, but it is virtually impossible individually to create synthetic fabric.
- Make lists of how you and other family members operate as consumers and producers.

Extensions

- Explore the concept of inventions as the development of new products to meet consumer needs.

- Brainstorm ideas for new products.
- Discuss the concept of patents and royalties for new ideas.
- Visit museums and historical reconstructions where earlier production techniques are displayed and demonstrated.

Chapter 10

Computers

Computer applications are available for all age ranges. Depending on the community one lives in, the preschool child has access to a computer at home, school, and in the public library. It is wise that the child learn how to operate a computer and use it as a tool early on. As with other skills, practice leads to improved productivity. Computer use contributes to basic reading and math skills, encourages the exploration of writing, motivates through creative open-ended programs, and incorporates decision-making and thinking skills. One can control independent computer use by young children by allowing them access only to appropriate programs and files.

Computer literacy has become a basic expectation for success in the twenty-first century. Therefore, young children need to begin developing literacy in this area early on. If you focus on utility programs rather than programs that are quickly outgrown, you will advance your child's computer literacy. Programs in which the child creates graphics and text to express ideas promote greater learning than those limited to matching, clicking and dragging, or shooting down objects.

MOUSE SKILLS

Learning how to use a mouse to point, click, and drag is a first step toward independent use of computers. Although there are special mice and keyboards designed for young children, they can also use standard mice and keyboards. Many programs designed for the very young require no reading but instead depend on the child's intuitive curiosity to click on visual prompts to see what will happen. Such exploratory behavior is rewarded with animation and sound, elements that encourage continued interaction.

Prerequisite Skills

- Awareness of the computer as a source of interest.
- Sense of the relationships among up, down, right, left, on, off, and so on.
- The willingness to use and not abuse the computer, recognizing that it may not be treated as an expendable toy.

Concepts

- There is a connection between how you move the mouse and the movement of the cursor on the screen.
- Clicking the mouse selects an object on the screen.
- Holding the mouse key down allows you to "drag" an object around the screen.
- There is a connection between releasing the mouse and placing the object on the screen.

Materials

- A computer equipped with a mouse.
- Suitable, age-appropriate programs for the computer.

Procedures

- Begin with a program such as *Mouse Practice* or other tutorials to introduce the skills needed to use a computer mouse.
- Have the child practice until the eye-hand coordination is sufficient to permit success when using other programs.

Extensions

- Apply mouse-handling skills to other age-appropriate programs.

KEYBOARDING

Programs for the very young incorporate only a minimal number of keys on the keyboard, such as the arrow keys, enter or return, and occasionally a letter to stand for a function. Once the child is ready to enter text, however, the layout of the entire keyboard becomes important. There is a difference of opinion regarding when and how it is appropriate to introduce touch typing. The one view is to avoid the need to break bad habits initially learned through hunt and peck methods. The other is to develop a sense of need to be able to enter text efficiently through experiences with trying to use the keyboard to write. In either case, once the child feels the need to master the keyboard, use of touch-typing programs becomes beneficial. Initial isolated practice is often frustrating and produces small gains. As the child begins to use the keyboard to enter text, you can give guidance that prepares the child for touch-typing skills. For example, have the child pretend there is a wall between the left and right hands so the child must use the proper hand for the proper half of the keyboard. Use at least one finger on each hand and begin to recognize location of letters in the top, middle, bottom rows and right or left side. Use the thumb for the space bar; use shift instead of caplocks for capital letters. As skill develops, involve additional fingers.

Prerequisite Skills

- Recognition of letters and symbols.
- Fine-motor control and eye-hand coordination sufficient to hit the desired key.
- Interest in creating written passages.

Concepts

- There is a standard layout for the location of symbols on a keyboard.
- To produce a capital letter, or the upper symbol on a key, one must use the shift key.
- To produce a space between symbols, such as between words or sentences, one must use the space bar.
- Specific keys produce punctuation marks.
- The delete key is used like an eraser to make corrections.

Materials

- Word processing program on a computer.

Procedures

- Begin by having the child dictate a story while you keystroke it.
- With the child sitting on your lap, guide their fingers to select appropriate keys.
- Encourage the child to create stories independently. Advocate the use of invented spelling so you focus on what the child has to say rather than on the mechanics of spelling, punctuation, and grammar.
- Print out the text and allow the child to illustrate it with crayons or markers.

Extensions

- Use a simple program to learn touch typing.
- Use a paint or draw program so the child can illustrate as well as write stories on the computer.
- Pair the correct spelling with the child's invented spelling version of a story to illustrate editing, and start establishing a sense of standard spelling. Take care not to let this approach discourage expression of ideas, which is the whole point of allowing invented spelling.

BASIC COMPUTER VOCABULARY

Part of computer literacy comprises knowing appropriate computer vocabulary. From the beginning, introduce the child to correct terminology to allow for easy conversations with other computer users. New terms are always being added to the vocabulary, but for the most part the child needs to be acquainted with terms for the parts of the computer, peripherals, and standard commands for navigating programs.

Prerequisite Skills

- The knowledge that things have names.
- An interest in using the computer.

Concepts

- Specialized vocabulary identifies components of the computer system.
- Commands and directions also have specific terms to identify them.

Materials

- List of terms such as monitor, keyboard, mouse, mouse pad, modem, printer, CD, CD drive, disc, disc drive, hard drive, cursor, menu, file, program, click, point, drag, highlight, delete, e-mail, web site, bookmark, button, icon.
- Labels to identify components of the system if desired.

Procedures

- Use standard terminology when talking about computer activity—for example, use "cursor" rather than calling it "the blinky thing" or "the arrow."
- Practice identifying the parts of the computer in game fashion by asking the child to point to or find a particular piece.

Extensions

- Integrate additional terminology as you encounter them—surge protector, URL, zip drive, downloading, networking, fonts, spell checker, edit, graphics, clip art—and on and on.

Chapter 11

Computer Programs, Formats, and Uses

The format of the computer program influences how much the child can learn. As with all products, manufacturers' claims need to be carefully evaluated. Programs that focus on providing drill and practice in a structured game format are more limited than those that foster creativity and inventive applications. The child will quickly lose interest in a repetitive structured format, which is outgrown as soon as the required skill is mastered. Programs through which the child creates products dependent on creativity and thinking processes hold the interest of the child much longer. Designing or thinking of applications that meet the instructional needs of the moment is the responsibility of the adult/teacher. Providing open-ended prompts gives the needed structure as well as challenge to the child to become a creative problem solver.

DRILL AND PRACTICE/GAME FORMAT

The strength of these programs lies largely in how well they motivate children to engage in practicing rote skills. They provide patient, repetitive practice and feedback related to learning basic skills such as math facts, letter sounds, and spelling. Weaknesses include their reliance on rote learning rather than on understanding and applying rules. Frequently, graphics that indicate incorrect answers are more appealing than those for correct answers, which leads some students to choose inappropriate responses on purpose.

Prerequisite Skills

- Whatever prerequisite skill is required to run the program. For example, rhyming words require an understanding of letter sounds; math facts involving regrouping require prior understanding of place value.

Concepts

- The focus tends to be on recall rather than developing and understanding concepts. For example, drill and practice of multiplication facts is more concerned with giving rapid correct answers than with understanding the concept of what happens when using the multiplication process.

Materials

- Drill-and-practice computer programs.

Procedures

- It is important to match the skill the child needs to practice with the content of the computer program. Time spent practicing skills already mastered or attempting skills that are beyond the child's current capabilities is time wasted.
- Follow the directions provided with the program.

Extensions

- Set levels of difficulty or timing features to increase the challenge to the child.
- Use the teacher edit feature to design a personalized practice for the child.

DISCUS BOOKS

Electronic versions of story books assist in learning to read by allowing the child to interact with the computerized version of the story. With these highly motivational programs, the child can listen to familiar stories, rearrange the sequence of events, manipulate visuals on the screen, initiate animation and sound effects, and in some cases rewrite sections of the story. The entertainment value of the program allows the child to enjoy the repetition of a favorite story. The reader is a skilled actor whose voice and inflection enhance the reading/listening experience, but one can alternate between activating the sound or reading the text independently.

Prerequisite Skills

- Mouse skills to make selections within the program.
- Attention span sufficient to interact with the program.

Concepts

- Stories are a sequence of events.
- Stories tell the actions and reactions of characters.
- Stories have a setting that identifies the time and place in which the story occurs.
- Stories frequently contain a problem or a conflict which needs to be resolved.

Materials

- A variety of discus book titles.

Procedures

- Follow the program directions and interact with the story.

Extensions

- Expand into using nonfiction titles in this format.

CREATE A BOOK FORMAT

These programs encourage and permit children to write and illustrate their own stories and to print them out in book format. Typically programs of this type give a choice of backgrounds, clip-art graphics to place on the selected background, and the opportunity to write text to accompany or explain each visual created. The finished product can be saved to a disc for later playback or printed out to create a book by stapling the pages together.

Prerequisite Skills

- A sense that a story has a beginning, middle, and end.
- Understanding that a book uses pictures and words to tell the story.
- Sufficient computer literacy skills to navigate the program.

Concepts

- The background illustration reflects the setting of the story.
- There is a similar relationship between the clip art used and the characters that participate in the story.
- The text matches or expands the content of the illustration.
- To develop an interesting story there needs to be some sort of conflict or problem the characters must solve.
- Pages of the book communicate best when fundamental principles of layout are followed.

Materials

- A create-a-book program.
- Disc to save on.
- A printer to create a hard copy of the book.

Procedures

- Practice learning to navigate the program to discover its potential.
- Follow the structure of the program to produce finished products.
- Save the story to disc and/or print it out.

Extensions

- Evaluate the finished product, identifying potential improvements for future products.
- Use book-making segments in content-oriented programs such as Edmark's *Imagination Express Series*, which has programs related to castles, rainforests, oceans, and neighborhoods.

THINKING SKILLS/DECISION-MAKING PROGRAMS

Programs of this sort give the child the chance to acquire and practice thinking skills and strategies for interpreting and organizing information. Skills such as sequencing, categorizing, identifying attributes, using grid coordinates, graphing, reading maps, and telling time form the basis of the activities. The child confronts a variety of situations that require the application of these skills. The range of variation in presentation increases the usefulness and the transferability of skills being learned. The skill concepts tend not to be content specific.

Prerequisite Skills

- Basic computer literacy level to permit navigation of programs.
- Background knowledge to make activities meaningful.

Concepts

- Strategies and thinking skills play a part in organizing and interpreting information.
- Good decisions are based on acquiring and interpreting accurate information.
- Thinking is fun.

Materials

- Programs such as *Thinking Things, Sammy's Science House, Trudy's Time and Place House, Graph Club, Tabletop Jr., Changes Around Us, Animals in Their World,* and *Carmen Sandiego Junior Detective Edition.*

Procedures

- Have the child interact with computer programs. The scope and purpose of selected programs follow:
- *Thinking Things'* activities supply practice in pattern recognition, auditory discrimination, and identifying attributes.
- *Sammy's Science House* incorporates sequencing, categorizing, recognizing the relationship between parts and the whole, and identifying seasonal attributes.

- *Trudy's Time and Place House* includes geographic concepts and map skill activities, along with practice in setting and reading both analog and digital clocks.
- *Graph Club* centers on the skills required for creating and interpreting graphs. Data are entered in table format and can be transferred into a variety of graphing formats, including pictograph, bar, circle, and line presentations.
- *Tabletop Jr.* focuses on creating and organizing data. You can create a population composed of individual characters, each of which can differ according to four variables (Populations of Party Hats vary according to color, shape, ribbons, and pompoms, while those of Snoods vary according to hair style, eyes, color of nose, and type of shoes). Once the population has been created, you establish rules for organizing them by attributes in one of six ways: bunching, graphing, grid coordinates, Venn diagrams, linking, and neighboring tiles. The rules can be hidden so that the child has to deduce them from the display, or the rule can be entered and population organized by the child to be checked for accuracy by the computer.
- *Changes Around Us* provides a database of pictures and information. The section related to seasons lets the user select animals, clothing, plants, water, or activities. The life-cycle section provides information related to nine animals and six plants. In addition to the database feature, the CD includes game activities and a multimedia production component.
- *Animals in Their World* uses a database format to provide pictures and information about fifty-eight animals, with nine items of information for each animal.

The CD also has game activities and a multimedia production component.

- *Carmen Sandiego Junior Detective Edition* does not require reading, but focuses on the use of strategies, memory, and matching skills. The player receives clues related to agricultural products, geographical features, landmarks, architecture, sports, and cultural events reflecting seven regions of the world. You get on-screen help in tracking down Carmen and members of her gang.

Extensions

- Programs that offer greater sophistication include *Tabletop*, which allows you to create a database that can be shown as icons and arranged in ways similar to *Tabletop Jr.*; and *Cruncher*, which is a spreadsheet program designed for student use.
- Other programs in the *Carmen Sandiego Series* provide clues to solving problems in various geographical and historical contexts.

PAINT/PRESENTATION PROGRAMS

Programs of this sort provide tools to create visuals. Typically these programs include line, box, circle, special effects, clip-art type stamps, and text tools as well as color and texture. You can import graphics and text from other sources and add sound to create multimedia presentations. Programs vary in their degree of sophistication from simple linear sequences of still pictures with or without sound, to complex presentations with animation, video clips, and branching capabilities. These programs are totally open ended: the only limit is your imagination.

Prerequisite Skills

- The ability to use storyboard planning, to synchronize the visual and text or visual and sound, to sequence topics within a presentation.
- Eye-hand coordination using a mouse.
- Recognition of functions represented by icons in the tool box.

Concepts

- One needs to organize the content of a presentation to maximize communication of one's message.
- Interesting packaging maintains the interest of viewers.
- Principles of layout and design impact the ability of the presentation to communicate the desired message.
- Too many font styles, sizes, and colors detract from the effectiveness of the delivery.

Materials

- Paint/presentation program.
- Access to sources for importing graphics, text, and sound.

Procedures

- Using a program, such as *Kid Pix*, introduce the user to one tool at a time providing time to explore and experiment. Youngest children can learn to use the stamp tool to place graphics, select the paint bucket and a color to fill in areas within the picture, use the text tool to spell words, or explore the special effects of the paintbrush tool. Freehand drawing with the mouse and pencil tool can be frustrating until eye/hand and mouse coordination is developed. Learning to manipulate stamps first reduces the frustration level.

- Provide a prompt describing a task and permit the child to try to create a response that matches the criteria of the prompt. For example, 1) draw a line across the middle of the screen; 2) make the top part blue and the bottom part green; 3) select stamps of things that are associated with the sky and the ground to be placed in the appropriate section. Or, at a more sophisticated level, ask the child to create a building using only the box tool. An older child might be asked to create a cityscape rather than a single building.

- The motivation of using the drawing tools is enhanced when there is an added element of problem solving. Give the child time to explore and discover the possibilities of the program by creating visuals that reflect personal interest. The potential of the program, however, is not limited to undirected creative play. With adult supervision and direction, you can add in an element of information handling. For example, activities that require the child to categorize or sequence stamps according to criteria retains the fun element but expands learning. Similar approaches can focus on utilization of other tools.

Extensions

- The use of shells or templates to provide a structure or format that the child can fill in with responses which meet the criteria of a given prompt saves a lot of time. The young child lacks the coordination to create a template, but can profit from repeated use of the format. For example, when learning the numbers one to ten, the child can place stamps in the appropriate boxes while they may be unable to create the boxes. Saving templates onto a disc and loading a file as needed makes it easy to provide repeated practice with minimal adult interaction. Moreover, by providing the structure for the activity, the student can focus on the content and ways to manipulate information.
- Use the slide show feature of *Kid Pix* to present a sequence of files.

CONTENT-SPECIFIC CD-ROMs

Content, as opposed to game type, CD-ROMS provide multimedia information on an ever-increasing number of subjects. The range is from general encyclopedias and broad reference databases to highly specialized and focused topics such as musical instruments, dangerous animals, and coral reefs. The interactive format encourages the child to learn about the subject area, and the CD-ROMs often have video clips that show motion and special effects that help in the comprehension of difficult concepts. Sound clips might provide the sound of a famous person's voice, a volcano eruption, a storm in action, animals and birds, musical excerpts—the possibilities are endless. Such "authentic" experiences enhance learning. The built-in search engines and hot buttons allow learners to follow their own thought patterns instead of complying with a prescribed path. One browses a CD in much the same way one leafs through a book.

Prerequisite Skills

- Basic handling of CDs and the loading procedure required.

Concepts

- CDs can contain pictures, sound, and video clips as well as text.
- One can select special features by clicking on appropriate icons.
- Information can be explored based on an individual word, broad topic, or a combination of terms.

Materials

- CD-ROMs.

Procedures

- Select and interact with CDs of your and the child's choice.

Extensions

- Learn more about the use of Boolean logic in applying search strategies.

A Final Thought

Experiences children have during their preschool years impact their later success in formal school settings. In fact, children who have not been introduced to preschool learning and language skills begin very quickly to fall behind their classmates who had such exposure. It is only through contact with concept development, and experience with books, writing materials, and verbal interactions, that the child enters school with an equitable chance for success. Furthermore, what happens during these formative years will play a major role in the child's success as an adult.

A child's primary requirement for success in school is regular interaction with an interested adult who takes the time to talk with and explain what can be learned by observing day-to-day activities. Take advantage of public services (parks, libraries, museums, etc.) to expand horizons. You don't need to purchase specialized or expensive materials. You just need an awareness of how to transform daily life into learning experiences and the ability to communicate to the child that all living experiences are learning experiences when they are connected, enlarged, and followed up on.

This type of involvement benefits a child throughout school and should not stop once formal education begins. It is key for the child to have a significant adult caring about school and providing encouragement and support. These mentoring partnerships repay both parties. Although time consuming, they are fun, and watching a child discover a concept or master a skill is rewarding to both the learner and the "teacher." The authors hope the material in this book will help foster interest in and understanding of how to provide this type of support for all children.

Bibliography

ASSOCIATIONS

Invent America, 518 King Street, Alexandria, VA. 703-684-1836.

BOOKS AND PERIODICALS

Barrett, Judi. *Cloudy with a Chance of Meatballs*, New York: Simon & Schuster, 1978.

Begley, Sharon. "Your Child's Brain," *Newsweek*," February 19, 1996, pp. 56-58.

Briggs, Raymond. *Jim and the Beanstalk*, New York: Coward, 1970.

Calhoun, Mary. *Hot Air Henry*, New York: Wm. Morrow, 1981.

Friedman, Ina R. *How My Parents Learned to Eat*, Boston: Houghton Mifflin, 1984.

Hanford, Martin. *Where's Waldo?* Boston: Little Brown, 1987.

How Things Work, New York: Time-Life Books, 1985.

Hutchins, Pat. *The Doorbell Rang*, New York: Greenwillow Books, 1986.

Jonas, Ann. *Round Trip*, New York: Greenwillow Books, 1983.

Lord, John Vernon. *Giant Jam Sandwich*, Boston: Houghton Mifflin, 1972.

Macaulay, David. *The Way Things Work*, Boston: Houghton Mifflin, 1988.

Mancini, Gail Hinchion. "Advice to the Voter," *Indiana Alumni* May/June 1996, p. 24.

Manguel, Alberto and Gianni Gualdalupi. *The Dictionary of Imaginary Places*, New York: Macmillan, 1980.

Salter, Christopher L., et al. *Key to the National Geography Standards*, Washington, D.C.: National Geographic Society, 1995.

Tolhurst, Marilyn. *Someboy and the Three Blairs*, New York: Orchard Books, 1991.

Usova, George M. *Efficient Study Strategies*, Pacific Grove, Calif.: Brooks/Cole, 1989.

Wolfe, A. as told to Jon Scieszka. *True Story of the Three Little Pigs*, New York: Viking, 1989.

COMPUTER SOFTWARE WITH SOURCES

Discus books, a term for a type of computer program produced by a number of publishers.

Kid Pix
Tabletop and *Tabletop Junior*
Carmen Sandiego Junior Detective Edition

Available from: Broderbund, P.O. Box 6125, Novato, CA 94948-6125.

Cruncher
Available from Davidson & Associates Inc., P.O. Box 2961, Torrance, CA 90509-2961.

Imagination Express Series
Sammy's Science House
Thinking Things
Trudy's Time and Place House
Available from Edmark, 6727 185th Ave. NE, Redmond, WA 98073-9721.

Animals in Their World
Change Around Us
Available from Raintree/Steck-Vaughn, P.O. Box 26015, Austin, TX 7875.

Graph Club
Available from Tom Snyder, 80 Coolidge Hill Rd., Watertown, MA 02171-2817.

Index

About the Authors

M. Ellen Jay is an elementary school library media teacher in Montgomery County, Maryland. Her background in curriculum and instructional design has been coupled with that in library and information science. She shares her experience working with children and school librarians in training through her writings and workshops, as well as serving as an e-mail mentor.

She enjoys travel so vacations have taken her to many countries worldwide as well as throughout the US. These adventures often suggest a theme for next year's lessons. Spare personal moments are spent reading, playing French horn, water gardening, or hiking.

Hilda L. Jay is a retired high school library media teacher who is delighted to have both of her daughters find pleasure in pursuing careers as school librarians. She continues to accept adjunct assignments and frequently volunteers time at Ellen's nearby school . . . just to keep up with the times. Her part of this writing team is doing research, editing, and the computer keyboarding. Since there is concurrence regarding philosophy and goals, writing together is mostly peaceable.